GW01279561

The Racing PORSCHES R to RSR

John Starkey

A **FOULIS** Motoring Book
First published 1987

© John Starkey 1987

All rights reserved. No part of this book may be reproduced or transmitted in any form or by any means, electronic or mechanical, including photocopying, recording, or by any information storage or retrieval system, without permission of the publisher.

Published by:
Haynes Publishing Group
Sparkford, Near Yeovil, Somerset
BA22 7JJ

Haynes Publications Inc.
861 Lawrence Drive, Newbury Park,
California 91320 USA

British Library Cataloguing in Publication Data
Starkey, John
    Porsche : from RS to RSR.
    1. Porsche 911 automobile—History
    I. Title
    629.2'222   TL215.P75

ISBN 0-85429-604-2

Library of Congress Catalog Card No.
87-81697

Editor: Robert Iles
Page layout: Mike King
Printed in England by: J.H. Haynes & Co. Ltd.

Contents

Foreword		**4**
Introduction		**5**
Acknowledgements		**7**
Chapter 1	S to R to Ss	**9**
Chapter 2	RS 2.7	**22**
Chapter 3	RSR	**30**
Chapter 4	RS 3 Litre	**40**
Chapter 5	RSR 3.0	**52**
Chapter 6	Racing in Europe	**66**
Chapter 7	Racing in America	**94**
Chapter 8	Rallying	**102**
Chapter 9	Driving Porsche	**114**

Foreword

For a car to achieve true classic status, there has to be more to its make-up than simply competition successes achieved by an efficient piece of machinery. It needs perhaps an element of mystique, made of a degree of uncertainty concerning numbers built, of varying detail specifications, of driving characteristics that make demands, both rewarding skill and punishing the clumsy.

These are characteristics one can rarely associate with German cars, built with that Teutonic thoroughness for which they are renowned, and sadly they are also characteristics which are being increasingly designed out of the ultra-efficient cars of our modern generation. Like human beings, it's the little foibles and idiosyncrasies in an otherwise superb piece of engineering that catch the enthusiast's imagination, and adds the mystique that transforms the merely excellent into a true classic.

The Porsche 911, after nearly 25 years in existence, is still being developed and improved at Weissach, probably the most advanced automotive research and development centre in the World. This fact is, to the engineer, in itself a contradiction in terms, as the 911 is a sporting vehicle with an inherently incorrect design, namely a large engine over-hanging at the back. Yet this illogicality is the very secret of the 911's success, permitting as it does light and responsive steering and, more importantly in this age of ever increasing power outputs, excellent traction.

Of the many variations produced on the 911 theme, the RS stands alone as the ultimate expression of 911 motoring, alive, responsive, immensely successful yet technically relatively simple. A 'Homologation Special' that turned into a limited series production run, it is little more than a road going competition car in concept, yet it is also a totally civilised and useable road machine, that even some 15 years after its inception can still achieve success on the race track. A true Classic in the best sense of that word.

As a fellow RS owner and driver, and also a fellow competitor in both hill-climbing and circuit racing, John Starkey is certainly well qualified to write this book, the first serious attempt at documenting the RS series. And like the 911 series itself, John too is something of an enigma, a deeply knowledgeable car enthusiast on many marques and eras, yet a cheerfully mad-cap extrovert who seems ever untroubled by the cares of this world.

On behalf of all my fellow RS fanatics at the 'Farm', may I wish you fellow fanatics happy browsing.

Josh Sadler
Autofarm Ltd

Introduction

I watched out of my window with expectant curiosity as the green Carrera came to a halt in the drive and the tall figure of John Broad emerged.

For years knowledgeable drivers had been telling me just how wonderful 911 Porsches were to drive (though tinged with dire warnings of what happened if you let the tail drift out too far or backed off the throttle in the middle of a corner) but up till then, (1983) I had had no opportunity to find out.

John Broad came into the house. "This is a delightful machine" he said. "A 3-Litre Targa Carrera. It may already be seven years old and have 85,000 miles on the clock but it's beautiful. Do come and try it."

I should explain that John has owned over 200 high performance cars in his lifetime including such beauties as a Ferrari 250 G.T. "Tour De France", a Short Wheelbase model, two or three 300 S.L. Mercedes and a Ford G.T.40, so his opinions on cars are not to be taken lightly!

Wandering out and climbing into the car, I was immediately impressed.

The green tartan of the seats had lasted well. In fact, had I been told that this car had only 15,000 miles on its odometer, I would have found it believable.

A turn of the key and the engine started immediately with that sharp intensity which only the best designed engines possess. Dipping the slightly odd feeling over centre clutch and engaging reverse, I backed out of the drive. Facing the right way, I now engaged 1st gear and drove off. The first thing to strike me was the wonderful steering. Surely no car before or since can rival a 911 in the sheer sensitivity of feel this imparts to the car's driver. I can only liken it to being able to trace over the road with your own hands. Then there was the performance. Even by 1984 there could be few cars to rival the Carrera's on-road go. The legendary traction simply catapulted the car away from every halt with no hesitation whatsoever and all accompanied by that soul stirring wail from the flat-six engine behind me. After all the horror stories of bad handling due to its rear mounted engine, I was astonished to find the handling supremely amenable. Yes, I felt sure that at extreme cornering velocities the car would spin backwards off the road, but I also felt that you would have to drive the car like a maniac to achieve these same speeds.

Four years have passed by and in that short period my wife and I have owned five 911s. All Carreras and the last three being particularly interesting. The first was a 3 litre RS Replica built up by Autofarm complete with 280 bhp. engine and the second a real RS 3.0. This a heavily compaigned (for this, read "worn-out"!) car which had won the group 4 G.T. class at Le Mans 1976 and had then been raced year after year until finally being imported into Britain. Of course, "Muggins" had to buy it and then set about the task of a running restoration. i.e. rebuild engine, straighten chassis etc. We are most of the way there as I write. The third car is a strange one. It started life as an RS 2.7 but was uprated to G-series RS 3.0 litre by the factory in 1978. It also has a full RSR spec. engine of 3.2 litres which gives a reputed 350 bhp!

It is the R, RS and RSR racing variants which interest us in this book. I firmly believe them to be the spiritual successors to the glorious 250 G.T. Ferrari Berlinetta which raced between 1955 and 1964. They won every victory for which they were eligible and the Porsche 911 RS and RSR achieved the same between 1973 and 1976, the years they were eligible for competition in the G.T. Class. Both were lightweight 2-seater coupes with up to 3-litre engines and both could be driven to the race track, change wheels and tyres, win and be driven home again, particularly with the RS variants. (Though this does not apply to RSR variants). Today the 2.7 RS is racing again and showing a clean pair of wheels to all the opposition in the "Pirelli" Porsche series of club races. 3-litre RSs are banned as it is thought they would too easily win! These are stupendous cars if you are an enthusiast and it is for those who love driving a highly individual car that this book is written.

Acknowledgements

To compile a book such as this, one needs a lot of help. It's sometimes a good job that we start projects without realizing quite how much help they will need, as I have the feeling that we sometimes wouldn't start at all!

The other thing that happens when you write a book is that you make a lot of friends and meet some exceedingly interesting people. When I first started this book, I realized that an American who I knew and had lived in Britain for many years, had once told me that he used to race Porsche RSRs at Le Mans. This was John (Jay) Rulon-Miller and it turned out that he had kept every piece of paperwork from those years together with a tremendous recall of events. I do thank him for all his assistance. Another American who helped fill in a lot of gaps, particularly with knowledge and information on the 911R was Kerry Morse, a resident of Tustin, California whose total Porsche knowledge is breathtaking.

The factory, of course, was the next place to which to turn and Gerd Schmidt who had overseen the building of the RSRs was a tremendous help, insisting that I met and talked with the head of Racing at Weissach, Herr Norbert Singer. Dagmar, Jurgen Barth's secretary, gave me free rein to all the racing department's files and her coffee did me the power of good! Thanks, Dagmar.

In Cologne, I met and interviewed the Kremer brothers, Manfred and Erwin. From what was only going to be a twenty minute interview, they allowed their enthusiasm for the 911 to run away with them and my visit lasted almost a whole day! It culminated with their bringing out the beautifully restored "Vaillant" RSR for me to photograph.

Someone who had driven for both the factory and the Kremer Brothers was John Fitzpatrick, probably the most successful of the G.T. class drivers of his day and he very kindly allowed me to interview him at his home in Spain where he now lives.

Back in England and that man who says he could talk Porsches for ever, Nick Faure, very kindly lent me his racing photographs and filled in many gaps on the RS 3.0. I must also thank Peter Lovett who let my good friend, Frank Bott photograph his RSR 3.0 and the Midland Motor Museum at Bridgenorth for allowing me to photograph Bill Stephen's similar car.

Alan Baker, the present owner of the ex-AFN RS 3.0 demonstrator and a lovely RS 2.7 Carrera lightweight was similarly good enough to help, not only with photographs but also with information which he had built up over the years whilst Charles Ivey filled out a lot of information concerning his years entering Le Mans with RSRs. Barry Robinson helped similarly with club racing in Britain whilst P.C.T. in Birmingham allowed me to photograph an RS 3.0 they were restoring.

Obtaining photographs which help to tell the story of older racing cars is always a thrill and here I am indebted not only to the Factory, but also to LAT Photographic who, as suppliers to *Motoring News* and *Motor Sport* supplied excellent pictures of the cars in Rallying and the European G.T. Championship as well as the World Championship for Makes.

Maurice Ouvier from France sent me photographs of my own RS 3.0 in the form in which it won its class at Le Mans and I am much indebted for them.

John Matta supplied photographs of his restored RS 2.7 as did Michael Burt, whilst John Moores supplied photographs of the RS 2.7 rallying.

Those doyens of Autofarm, Josh Sadler and Steve Carr, were kind enough to help me with information on the RSs. Josh also supplied the Foreword.

I cannot leave this page without thanking that superb racing driver and journalist, Paul Frere, who drove so many of the Porsche factory cars at their invitation because of his unique combination of talents. He graciously gave me permission to reproduce his impressions of driving the works-entered 1973 Martini-sponsored RSR.

Chapter 1

S to R to Ss

The story of the racing versions of the Porsche 911 really begins with the 911R which was a "full house" attempt by the factory to see how far they could go with a lightened 911 (830 kilogrammes) and with a much more powerful engine. Let's explain the meaning of this chapter's title. Ever since the introduction of the basic 911, in 1964, Porsche customers had wanted more power and performance and so, in 1967, Porsche announced the 911S. The engine was tuned to produce 160 bhp as against the standard car's 130 bhp by giving it larger valves, modified cylinder heads, camshafts with more overlap, forged 'slipper' pistons, soft-nitrided connecting rods and a smaller diameter cooling fan. 40IDS Weber carburettors with high-speed enrichment were used. An anti-roll bar was fitted at the rear (as well as at the front) and Koni dampers were specified.

New ventilated brake discs were fitted all round and the "S" now weighed 50 kilogrammes less than the standard car. The rev limit was raised to 7,300 rpm and a rev limiter cut out the ignition when this engine speed was reached. Top speed was now quoted as 140 mph instead of the standard 2-litre car's 131 mph.

These were the main points from which the factory developed the 911R, but because the factory did not make the 500 sufficient to homologate the car in the G.T. class, it was forced to run as a prototype and therefore only a small batch of 24 were made. Because of this classification, the factory eventually lost interest in the project. However, the lessons learned from the "R" were used in all the G.T. racing versions of the 911 which followed.

The "R" (for *rennen*, meaning race) had its body made by Karl Bauer, a body manufacturer in Stuttgart who worked in association with the factory. Its main points of difference with the normal production model were as follows: front wing (fenders), front and engine cover were made from glass reinforced plastic, as were the front and rear bumpers top and bottom of the dashboard and even the tail-light assemblies! The doors were in aluminium. The floorboards were drilled: "like swiss cheese" whilst all hinges were in aluminium and the rear wings were bulged out slightly to accommodate seven inch rims, whilst at the front, six inch width rims were used. These were Fuchs pattern wheels, as on the 911S.

The thickness of the rest of the bodywork's metal was as the standard car as the factory were keen to retain the stiffness of the production car. Plexiglass was used in all the side windows with some very pretty louvres being let into the tops of the rear quarter windows, whilst the front quarter lights were fixed with circular ventilators. The rear window was made of a substance called "Plexidur" and was 2 mm thick whilst the windscreen was of 4 mm thick glass. An oil cooler (a serpentine shape) for the engine was fitted in the right front wing whilst its connections to the engine were led through the sills.

Inside the car the obvious lightening moves of doing away with the rear seat squabs, heater, ashtray and cigar lighter were employed whilst only the sun visor above the driver's side was kept. Mounted in the dashboard were the speedometer, the 10,000 rpm tachometer and one combined dial showing oil pressure and temperature. No clock was fitted whilst the horn button was moved from the centre of the steering wheel (this a "Monza" item) to the dashboard.

A ventilated bucket seat made by Scheel was fitted for the driver and a

A fine study of Toine Hezemans 911S racing in England in 1968

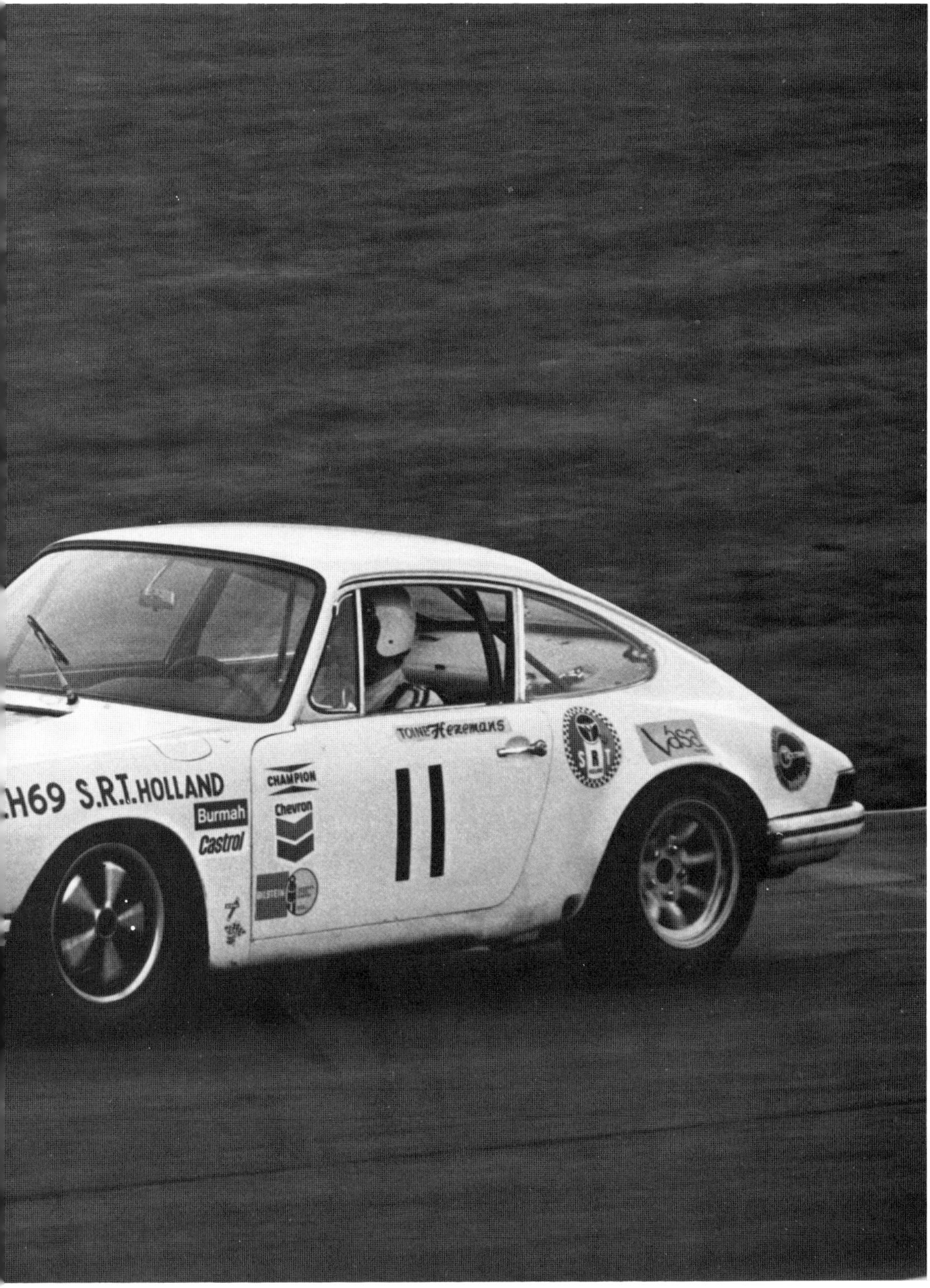
H69 S.R.T.HOLLAND
Burmah
Castrol
CHAMPION
Chevron
11

light plastic seat was furnished for the navigator/co-driver.

The gearbox was a 5-speed unit (type no 901/902) for which three sets of gears could be used. A "nurburgring" set was fitted at the factory. This selection of gears was mid-way between a low hillclimbing set and a high le Mans type.

A limited-slip differential was fitted together with a 7:31 crown wheel and pinion. A ratio of 6:31 was an option. The suspension was standard "S" but lowered. An oil tank made of aluminium was installed ahead of the rear axle and was filled via a cap fitted in the right-hand rear wing. There was no heater.

Standard colour was white and if you, (the customer) wanted another colour, this had to be specified three weeks prior to collection. The weight of the prototype car was 800 kilogrammes; customer cars were reputed to weigh 30 kilos more.

Four prototypes were built, chassis nos. 911307670, 911307671, 911305876 and 911306681. The "production" run, (if such it could be called) went from chassis no: 911899001 to 911899019. Series production cars were built in Autumn 1967.

A 22 gallon fuel tank, plastic or steel to order, was fitted with its filler recessed into the front lid. This piped its contents, via 2 Bendix fuel pumps, to the engine which has been listed as type 901/22.

This was a highly tuned 911 flat 6 with magnesium crankcase, though a lightweight aluminium one was used on some cars. Alloy cylinder heads and cylinders, these being chrome plated were employed, whilst compression ratio was 10.3 to 1.

Two plugs per cylinder were used, these being Bosch X270821 platinum type, 12 mm size. In 1977, a later owner of one of these cars complained that it cost US$600 just to change plugs! The ignition system (Marelli) was partly transistorised. Two three choke 46 IDA Weber carburettors were fitted whilst the forged crankshaft with different counterweights to accommodate higher speeds was mounted in eight bearings. Titanium connecting rods were used and an 840 watt alternator was fitted. Power was quoted at 210 bhp at 8,000 rpm. It would take Porsche just 5 years to introduce a production 911 with this power output for the road – the 2.7RS Carrera.

Some cars were fitted with the 901 321 engine which featured fuel injection by slides and was identical to the unit fitted in the 910 sports-racer.

500 cars were required to be built within twelve months to have the 'R" homologated as a G.T. car and race in that class. This idea was put forward by Huschke von Hanstein in October 1967, but the sales department replied that they did not believe the public would buy what was essentially a stripped racer. They were to be proved wrong in the case of the RS 2.7 Carrera.

One experimental engine was tried in the "R", this being a flat-six of 2-litres but with twin cams per bank of cylinders. It was type number 916. The factory say that this was more or less half of the projected flat-12 powerplant of the 917 sports-racer. It produced 230 bhp at 8,000 rpm but the works lost interest in the 'R" installation when all the entries in the "Tour de Corse" suffered engine trouble. Gerard Larrousse did use a semi-works entry in the Lyons-Charbonniere rally, however. It was chassis number 911899 005 and was purchased by Jo Siffert. It featured in the Steve McQueen film 'Le Mans' and is now in the USA.

All the above took place in 1967 and Porsche moved on to homologate the 911S in Group 3 (GT cars). They also homologated their bottom of the range 911T using a 911S engine, lightened bodywork and sports seats. The weight of this car was stated as 923 kilogrammes and as anti-roll bars did not come into the homologation process, this can be seen as a clever move by the factory to give themselves a light base for a group 3 car.

For these cars in racing versions, Porsche gave them 2-litre engines which, apart from their valve sizes of inlet 42 mm and exhaust 38 mm to comply with the rules, were virtually as per the sports-racing Carrera 6 prototypes. The ignition system was standard and an oil cooler was fitted into the right-hand front wing. Along with the Carrera 6's pistons, the compression ratio became 10.4 to 1 and ports and inlet manifolding became larger. For the 911T, Porsche even homologated titanium connecting rods!

A stronger clutch and lightened flywheel led to the 901/902 gearbox with various gear sets to choose from. In this connection, it should be pointed out that the second gear pinion was machined directly onto the mainshaft and the factory therefore offered a "competition" gearbox mainshaft with separate gear choice. The ring and pinion gear now had a limited slip differential of 50%, but this was increased later to one with an 80% locking factor.

For rallying, Porsche offered the 911L, homologated in group 2 (modified touring cars) and equipped with a "Rally" engine (200R) which was the standard 130 bhp engine modified with the addition of "S" camshafts and pistons and with 40 IDA Weber carburettors. Once again a lightened flywheel and stronger clutch were used, together with a "rally' exhaust system. With this specification, 160 bhp was claimed.

15 mm anti roll bars were fitted front and rear and Koni dampers were used.

With a "Sportskit", (available from the factory) power could be increased further in two stages. In stage 1, 36 mm diameter carburettor chokes were available with harder plugs whilst stage 2 reduced the back pressure of the exhaust system to give 165 bhp. It was normal to specify 6" front and 7" rear wheelrim widths though any width was available from 4.5" to 7". Wheel diameter was 15" and anti-roll bars of 14, 15 and 16 mm were available, once again, in any combination and the factory did suggest, naturally, the hardest setting of 16 mm bars all round for racing.

For 1970, Rico Steinemann, the racing manager had the 911S homologated in Group 4 (special GT class) and Group 3 (production GT class). He had already attempted to homologate the car in Group 2 (Touring cars) but the FIA had thrown this application out. For group 4, therefore, Steinemann was very clever and had the sample car submitted for

R to RSR PORSCHE

911R engine number 118 9 9013.
Serial number 5080012

inspection (and catalogued!) extensively lightened by using aluminium front lid and bumpers, wire mesh instead of a metal grille on the engine cover and stripping out the interior using plain doortrims with a leather pullstrap to open and close the doors. There was no glovebox lid and rally seats were used.

A larger tank, once again with the filler fitted flush with the front lid was supplied, complete with narrow spare wheel and the car was homologated at 840 kilogrammes! Very few of the GT class race cars ever got down to the minimum weight, however. One such exception was Gerard Larrousse's 2.4ST which he drove on the 1970 "Tour de France". Larrousse offered the factory engineers a bottle of champagne for every kilo they managed to remove from "his" car below the 800 mark.

By removing every last non-essential item and employing lots of drilling, the car finally finished up standing on its minilite wheels weighing in at 789 kilogrammes. Fitted with Weber carburettors, the engine gave 245 bhp at 8,000 rpm. Larrousse, however, had not bargained on the Matra V12 prototypes lasting the event, but they did, and pushed his entry down to 3rd place overall.

To backtrack a little: in 1969, Porsche introduced a longer wheelbase of 2,271 mm as against 2,211 mm to the 911 range to improve the weight distribution and, as a corollary, the handling of the car. As well as this modification, which was accomplished by moving the rear wheelarches back by 60 mm (2.24 inches) and lengthening the rear trailing arms of the suspension, the crankcase of the engine was now manufactured from magnesium instead of aluminium. This measure saved 22 lbs. During the production run of the "B" series, magnesium was also used for the gearbox housing, again replacing aluminium.

New rules now allowed the wheel arches to be extended a further 2" from standard to accommodate wider wheels and, beginning with the "C" series, the engine capacity was increased to 2,195 cc by increasing the bore to 84 mm. If Porsche could now increase the capacity of the engine by bore increase only, as per the regulations, they could run at the next class limit of 2.5 litres and they accomplished this in two stages.

First, the capacity of the engine was increased to 2,247 cc, an increase in the bore of just 1 mm per cylinder to 85 mm and the factory made use of "biral" cylinders. These consisted of cast iron cylinders with alloy fins bonded on. Twin ignition had now been homologated, though with normal coils and contact breakers, and this was part of the engine tune together with polished and crack-tested connecting rods.

Compression ratio on this model was 10.3 to 1. As before, standard valves were used, 46 mm for inlet and 40 mm for the exhaust size. Bosch twin-row, six-plunger pump (mechanical) injection was now being used in the production cars and this was modified with a space cam to match the Carrera 6 racing cams which were now installed. Tuned induction pipes without an air filter were added. The racing engine for group 4 could be had with Weber 46

IDA carburettors having 42 mm diameter choke tubes. Strangely, the power output of 230 bhp was the same for either version. The standard crankshaft and bearings were used. Thirty of these engines were built, the factory designating them type 911/20. For the thirty cars that were built to take these engines, the roof, parts of the floorpan and the scuttle were manufactured in thinner gauge steel than that used for the road cars. Cars retained and run by the factory employed even thinner steel for their doors. In March 1971, the bores were opened further to 87.5 mm and this increased the capacity to 2,381 cc. Output of this engine went up to 250 bhp, both versions achieving this peak power at 7,800 rpm. Torque values for these engines were 170.3 lbs/ft. for the 2.3 litre engine and 188.4 lb/ft. for the 2.4 litre engine, both at 6,200 rpm.

These racing versions, which were known internally as "ST", had body modifications which included thinner than standard metal for such parts as the seat pan back and side panels, the roof panel and both the rear side panels. Chasing the cause of lightness, the seat slide supports and the heater ducts were removed as were the seat belt anchorage points, the glove box lid and the ashtray. Missing also were the

The 911R in action

engine cover and front cover locks, (these being replaced with rubber fasteners), the sun visor, the front torsion bar protectors, the foglight recess covers and the rear torsion bar covers. There was no soundproofing or underseal and even the amount of paint used was kept to a minimum.

Further options from the factory in order to lose still more weight included a plastic front cover as well as front and rear bumpers made of the same material and aluminium skinned doors with steel frames of 0.75 mm thickness.

A transverse bar was fitted in the front compartment in between the front struts to aid stiffness in this area and fuel tanks of 17.6 or 24.2 gallons were available. For racing, 7" front and 9" rear wheel widths were used. Racing tyre sizes were 4.75/10.00 – 15 and 4.75/11.30 – 15 respectively. Plexiglass was available to replace all glass except for the windscreen which could be had with even thinner glass. The whole body package was finished off with Recaro sports seats being fitted.

For rallying, Porsche modified the engine only slightly by removing the air filter and skimming 0.5 mm off the heads, fitting a rally exhaust system and richening up the fuel/air mixture at the injection pump. As before, a lightened flywheel and stronger clutch were used. They quoted 190 bhp with this set up. Apart from the gearbox casing being made of magnesium, the box itself was a new, strengthened design designated type 911. As before, many combinations of ratios were offered and the final drive ratio could be 7:31 or 6:32. Each rear half-shaft employed two constant velocity joints, these also taking up the variation in length. 6" wheel rim widths were used in rallying with 185/70 VR15 tyres. For braking, ventilated discs with aluminium "S" calipers were used at the front whilst "M" steel calipers were at the rear. Linings recommended were Textar 1431 G for racing. Suspension was adjudged good enough by the factory to employ the same type of settings as for the 2-litre car, i.e. lower the car by adjusting the torsion bars and making available anti-roll bars of differing diameters.

To take complete advantage of the 2.5 litre class limit, Porsche supplied several sets of components for customers with engines of this size. In fact, they built two 2.5 engines of differing stroke/bore combinations due to a problem they encountered with the first design.

This design took advantage of the "E" production variant having a piston stroke increase to 70.4 mm from the previous 66 mm and now Porsche increased the bore to 86.7 mm. This resulted in a capacity at the class limit (2,494 cc). Otherwise its specification was as the 2.4 litre unit. In its new size, the engine now developed 275 bhp at 7,900 rpm and 196 lbs/ft. of torque at 6,200 rpm.

The problem with this engine was that it tended to loosen its flywheel bolts or, in extreme cases, break the crankshaft. There was little doubt at the factory that this was totally due to the longer stroke now being used and so some engines were built using the previous stroke of 66 mm whilst employing "Nikasil" cylinders with a bore of 89 mm. This resulted in the same power and torque figures of the long-stroke engine without its fragility.

A new gearbox, type 915, was offered with this racer, having a torque rating of 217 lb/ft, more than 20% higher than the type 911 gearbox which had reached its limit with the 2.4 litre car. An oil pump was now incorporated into the front cover of this gearbox and this sprayed jets of oil onto the gear clusters for

Year	Model Body Type	Chassis No	Engine type	Gearbox type	Cyl	Bore x stroke	Capacity	HP (DIN) at rpm	Torque (mkg) at rpm	Comp ratio	W'base (mm)	Track fr rear (mm)	Length (mm)	Weight (kg)
1965	Coupé 911-2.0 'Monte'	303075-076 303085	901/02	902/2	6	80x66	1991	160/6600	18,2/5200	9.8:1	2211	1367/1339	4163	1030
1967	Coupé 911S-2.0 'Rallye'	306655S-657S	901/30	901/30	6	80x66	1991	170/7300	18,5/5200	10:1	2211	1367/1339	4163	1030
1967	Coupé 911R-2.0	307670-671/ 305876 11899001R- 118990019R	901/22	901/54 901/50 90.53	6	80x66	1991	210/8000	21/6000	10.5:1	2211	1370/1370	4100	800
1970	Coupé 911S-2.2 2.2 'Rallye'	9110300001-003 9110300949-0950	911/02	901	6	84x66	2195	180/6500	20,3/5200	9.8:1	2268	1374/1355	4163	960
1970	Coupé 911S-2.3	9110300001-0003	911/20	901	6	85x66	2247	240/7800	23/6300	10.3:1	2268	1374/1355	4163	840
1970	Coupé 911S-2.4 'Proto'	911030949	911/21	901	6	85x70,4	2395	260/8000	25/6500	10.3:1	2268	1402/1421	4100	790
1971	Coupé 911S-2.2 'Safari'	9111300637 9111300683 9111300612 9113000589 9111300561	911/02	901	6	84x66	2195	180/6500	20,3/5200	9.8:1	2268	1374/1355	4163	980
1972	Coupé 911S-2.5	9112300041/047	911/73 911/70	915	6 6	89x66 86,7x70,4	2466 2492	275/8000 275/8000	26,5/6300 26,5/6300	10.3:1 10.3:1	2271	1402/1421	4147/960	

lubrication instead of the splash variety previously employed. This had absorbed 7 bhp at maximum speed and the distance between shaft centres was now 77 mm, whilst the first gear pinion was cut on the main shaft. This meant that this shaft had to be changed to alter the first gear ratio (if needed). In this gearbox, the opportunity was taken to move 1st gear from its previous left and back position to being forward in front of 2nd gear. Fifth gear was now to the right and forward with reverse situated directly behind 5th.

This was in response to road car drivers who complained about the racing type 1st – 2nd gear change associated with the previous 5-speed gearboxes. They much preferred 1st and 2nd gear selection in one plane.

The crown wheel and pinion ratios offered were now 7:31 or 7:37. On the "E" series, also, a small front air dam was mounted beneath the front bumper and the engine oil cooler was now mounted in the centre of this with its piping taken beneath the sill on the right-hand side.

The only change in the suspension was a move from Koni to Bilstein dampers and these were employed with, obviously, harder settings than on the road cars. From the factory, these G.T. racing cars cost DM 49,680.

911R, chassis no. 911508005 pictured in 1975. The car is thought to be ex-Larrousse

Chapter 2
RS 2.7

Right away, let's explain the meaning of the title "Carrera" as it features with the RS series of 911s. It came from the Carrera Panamerica series of races held in Mexico in the late 1940s and '50s. Translated literally it means "Race." Porsche did very well in this series, being 3rd overall and winning their class in 1954. Ever since they have reserved the name for a very special series of road cars. RS stands for *"Renn Sport"* – literally Motorsport.

By the end of 1973 the 917 and its Turbo derivative, the 917/30 had finished their all-conquering competitive careers, outlawed by swiftly made rule changes designed to stop the cars as they had steamrollered all opposition in both the world championship for sportscars and the Can-Am series. In the previous year, the factory had looked at the new rules likely to come into force from 1976 and realised that the 911, their current production road car, formed an admirable basis for these.

Dr. Helmuth Bott had been appointed Head of Development in 1972, replacing Ferdinand Piech and, as he had been closely associated with the 911's development from its inception, he made an ideal choice.

The problems facing him and the factory were these. The 2.4 litre 911S, the top of the range road car then in production was too heavy and as the homologation weight of a car was supposed to be the weight of a racing version, a new, lighter model was needed. Also, by 1973, more power was needed for the track. Bigger engined opposition in the shape of the new Ferrari Daytona and the V8 Ford engined De Tomaso Pantera were already threatening to win the G.T. class by sheer brute power over the 911's more nimble handling. Yet one more problem faced the 911 – aerodynamics. Approaching speeds of 150 mph the 911S, though equipped by now with a small air dam at the front, still exhibited lift at the rear, which, combined with 60% of the car's weight due to the rear mounting of the engine, caused less than desirable oversteer through fast bends.

The Carrera RS 2.7 was the result. On a basic 911 chassis the changes were as follows. Concerning the weight, the car was lightened by the use of thinner than standard metal for the doors, the roof, the luggage compartment lid, front wings, luggage compartment floor, the seat recess in the floorpan and even the gearstick platform! Thinner glass was provided by "Glaverbel" all round with the rear side windows fixed in their own special chrome frame, and most of the sound proofing went.

The carpet was black "needle felt" whilst the interior trim was reduced to a minimum, in particular rubber mats were used on the floor and the door trims simplified to a leather strap for the door opening and a small plastic handle to close the door. These were actually ex Fiat 500 parts! No clock or passenger sun visor was used. The rear "+2" seats were not fitted and lightweight bucket seats were installed for driver and passenger complete with head restraints and with thumbscrew adjustment to alter the rake up to 15°. The seats had to be slid forward to allow access to the rear seats. No underseal was used and only a low-tone horn fitted. The rest of the interior of the car was standard left-hand drive 911S, this including an instrument binnacle which featured, from the left, a gauge showing the fuel level in the 13.6 Imperial gallon tank located in the left-hand side and an oil level indicator in the right-hand side. Next to this was a similar gauge showing oil temperature on the left and oil pressure on the right. Alongside was situated the large tachometer directly in the line of sight of the driver. This read to 8,000 rpm and was red-lined at 7,300 rpm. A rev-limiter was employed to cut out the ignition at this engine speed.

The main beam tell-tale was placed at the bottom of this dial. Next to the tachometer was the speedometer complete with sidelights tell-tale. Underneath this binnacle across the dashboard were situated (again from left to right) the button to release the fuel flap, the knob for the rear window demister, the cigar lighter, the heater controls, the hazard lamps and tell-tale and the switch for the lights. The steering column sported two stalks, the one on the left operating the indicators, the dipswitch, headlight flasher and the parking lights whilst the right-hand one controlled the 3-speed windscreen wipers and the screen washers.

Further changes to the bodywork included the rear wheel arches being enlarged in order that the car could now use 7" wheel rims at the rear in conjunction with 6" rims at the front. More importantly, this now meant that with the addition of the 2" lateral extensions which were allowable under the CSI rules, 11' wheels could be fitted at the rear and 9" rims could be fitted at the front. 15" diameter wheels of forged aluminium alloy of the distinctive Fuchs "S" pattern were used. Tyres were Pirelli Cinturato CN36 or Dunlop SP D4 of 185/70VR15 at the front and 215 VR15 at the rear. 7 mm spacers were used to further widen the track at the rear.

Bumpers front and rear were in polyester with no trim except for colour-coded tape. A number plate support was built into the front spoiler. In the RSR version, specifically built for the racetrack, this became the intake to the engine oil cooler. No luggage

23

compartment light was fitted, but a compressed air bottle was supplied to blow up the 15" spacesaver tyre in the event of a puncture.

A note here on colours. The usual range of 25 Porsche colours was offered, ranging from Grand Prix white, (of course!) to black with colours such as signal-orange, viper-green and gulf-blue in between. No metallic colours were used due, no doubt, to the difficulty of making it adhere to glass reinforced plastic. The very first car off the line was orange. Thereafter Grand Prix white appears to have predominated with the Carrera side script being colour coded in red, green or blue to match the wheel centres. We have, however, seen one car which was originally purple!

A "duck's tail", (in German-*"Burzel"*) spoiler, in G.R.P with alloy inner frame on early cars and steel on later ones was used fitted with rubber quick-release clamps and this not only cut down weight still further but, much more importantly, it greatly reduced aerodynamic lift and actually added 2 mph to the top speed to give a claimed 153 mph.

Autocar tested a "touring" version (MYX 4L) at 149 mph so a lightweight version should have achieved the claimed speed easily. The engine differed from the 911S in the following particulars. New cylinder barrels having 15 instead of 11 cooling ribs were fitted but it was their interior, rather than their exterior which would show the greatest difference in the performance of the car. Instead of the cast-iron barrels being fitted with a "Biral" cylinder liner, the cylinders dispensed entirely with liners and instead had a layer of nickel-silicon deposited on them by means of electrolysis. This process, known as 'Nikasil" had been previously used on the 917 and enabled the bore to be taken out to 90 mm. Combined with the unchanged stroke of 70.4 mm this now gave the "Boxermotor" a capacity of 2,687 cc instead of the previous 2,341 cc. The new motor used the same compression ratio (8.5:1), valve timing, lift and port sizes as the 911S.

Pistons had a slightly flatter top whilst the Bosch fuel injection pump was uprated to cope with the increased demand made upon it and a new distributor with a modified advance curve was fitted. With these changes a maximum power output of 210 bhp (DIN) at 6,300 rpm was achieved compared with 190 bhp at 6,500 rpm from the 2.4 litre "S" engine. 159.5 lbs/ft of torque had come from this engine and the RS engine now gave 188.4 lb/ft at 5,100 rpm. All this was achieved on pump (2-star) fuel!

The plastic engine cover which ducted air from the fan around the cylinders was coloured a distinctive red on Carrera RSs. The gearbox was the type 915 5-speed unit as used in the 911S, but with 4th and 5th ratios raised slightly. Final drive being 7/31. Standard gear ratios were as follows: 1st: 11/35. 2nd: 18/33. 3rd: 23/29. 4th: 27/25 and 5th: 29/21. An oil pump, situated in the front cover, was driven by the output shaft. The factory claimed acceleration times of 0 to 62 mph in 5.8 seconds for a lightweight and 6.3 seconds for a "Touring" car. Paul Frere timed a lightweight at 13.0 seconds for the 0 to 100 mph sprint.

Suspension changes from 911S specification were as follows: Bilstein front struts replaced the previous Konis whilst an aluminium forging was utilized to support the rear of the front wishbones. The rear diagonal suspension arms were also strengthened around the rear wheel bearings and a bracket was employed to give increased support to the rear suspension transverse member. This was attached to the floorpan. Anti-roll bars were 15 mm at the front and rear.

We have given here a detailed look at the original lightweight specification (M471) of the 2.7RS. A "Touring" version (M472) could be specified and this incorporated 911S trim featuring such options as carpets, more soundproofing, openable rear windows, reclining Recaro front seats and "occasional" seats which folded to form a parcel shelf in the rear. A rear window wiper and stronger springs for the seats could even be ordered! The rear bumper was made of steel. In addition this version carried 2x36 Amp-hour 6-volt batteries, one on either side of the front mounted spare wheel whilst the "Sport" lightweight employed one 12-volt battery on the left-hand side. Torsion bar adjustment was actually more (at 36° 30") on "a touring" car than on a lightweight (33°). This was no doubt to help to set up a slightly heavier car. Cars after chassis no. 1036 appear to have received more underseal than previously particularly in the engine bay and under the luggage lid.

The RS was announced at the Paris motor show on October 5th 1972 and by November an astonished and delighted sales staff were able to report that the first 500, qualifying the car in group 4 (Special Grand Touring cars) had been sold. Another batch of 500 were quickly built and sold and this qualified the car to run in group 3 (Production Grand Touring cars). Chassis numbers run in the series 9113600001 to 9113601590. As in all 911s, there is a production number stamped into the dashboard behind the trim beneath the glovebox to fully identify the car. Engine numbers did not match the chassis numbers. They commenced at 6630021 for the first production car, 3600011 and finished at 6631550 in the fourth from last car made, 3601587. The first car was produced in July 1972 and the last one was finished in July 1973. A total of 1,580 Carrera RSs were made. The first ten cars in the series were retained by the works as prototypes.

111 cars came to Britain in right-hand drive form and 17 were genuine lightweights. They were fitted with steel fuel tanks instead of the plastic ones fitted to European specification cars. It's interesting to note that the "Touring" versions were usually trimmed to a higher specification than their European counterparts. Most received an electric sun roof and electric windows. According to factory figures, "Touring" versions (or RSTs, as they were known) weighed 1075 kilogrammes and a lightweight "Sport" version 960 kilogrammes.

Jerry Sloniger tested a lightweight RS 2.7 Carrera for the April 1973 issue of *"Road Test"*. An abridged version was also published in the Australian *"Sports Car World"* in February 1973.

The car Sloniger tested, registration

An RS 2.7 lightweight now fully restored

no: LB P 500, was tested at 0 to 60 mph in 5.7 seconds and 0 to 100 mph in 15.8 seconds. Top speed was given at 153 mph. This particular car had already been shunted by an ex-Porsche race driver within its first 1100 miles whilst the car which showed up for the photographs was one of the prototypes, registration no: LB ZH 43.

Sloniger wrote that the RS appeared so rapidly on the scene that perhaps the car ought to have had "Carrera" written backwards on the nose! He went on to say that the Bilstein dampers gave no tendency for the car to wander and he rated the precision of steering as "excellent".

Denis Jenkinson, *"Motor Sport"*'s famous continental correspondent wrote a piece for that magazine which was published in February 1973. He began the article by saying that ever since the 911 had begun, he had thought the car too big for its engine. Now, with the arrival of the RS 2.7, said Jenkinson, all this was cured at a stroke. He wrote that this car (MYX 4L) had "steam" as compared to "poke". The difference explained Jenkinson, was that the RS surged past slower traffic at over 100 mph on autobahns and motorways simply by flattening the accelerator in fifth gear. On a 911S, said "Jenks", you needed to change down for the same

'Coming for a ride daddy?' John Matta's beautifully rebuilt RS 2.7 Carrera in Italy where it now resides

effect and lost time. Jenkinson ran-in the car for the British Concessionaires and was told not to exceed 5,000 rpm to begin with. As this was equivalent to 110 mph in fifth gear, this, said Jenkinson, was no hardship!

As the car was being steadily run-in Jenkinson reflected that peak revs in 2nd, 3rd or 4th left his mind boggling slightly and that the acceleration in these gears was the standard for all to aim at.

He reported that the cornering potential of the car was so high that it was time for a different seat for a passenger to counter the G-forces and changes of direction that the RS was capable of, because the driver, being braced between the pedals and the steering wheel could anticipate them. The only part of the car that Jenkinson did not like was the gearchange. He had much preferred the old set up with 4th and 5th gears in the same plane instead of 5th gear being "out on a limb", particularly as the change back from 5th to 4th needed to be done with deliberation.

"Jenks" found the suspension on the harsh side, being conscious of every ripple and bump in the road but saying that this proved the Carrera had all four wheels planted firmly on the road and this was what made 911s so good on circuits such as the Targa Florio and the Nurburgring.

In conclusion, Dennis Jenkinson said that his instant reaction was "What an incredibly honest motor car" and, coupled with integrity in all walks of life, he found these to be desirable qualities.

Probably the most complete road test of all was that carried out by the *"Autocar"* and published in their May 1973 edition. The car involved was once again MYX 4L, the demonstrator which "Jenks" had run-in and so impressed were the testers that they headlined their test "sensational, even by Porsche standards". In their preamble the magazine reported that every one of the first five hundred cars had been ordered and that it was difficult to see how the factory could avoid making as many Carreras as possible. Not only was this the fastest road-going Porsche, it was also the most tractable.

After the technical description of the car, *"Autocar"* described its dynamics. They reported the engine springing into life with "stirring alacrity" and then went on to say how easy the car was to drive. Clutch pedal effort was low and the gear change was light. The magazine reported the RS to be more flexible than other 911s and they thought it might even be quieter!

The acceleration times of the car were outstanding, even by today's standards. Thirty mph from a standstill came up in 2.1 seconds, demonstrating the car's massive traction while 60 mph was reached in a staggering 5.5 seconds. 0 to 100 mph was recorded in just 15 seconds whilst even 0 to 130 mph took just over 30 seconds. Maximum speed was reached on a trip to Belgium and 149 mph was the result.

"Autocar" went on to say that to all intents and purposes, this performance was easy to use on the road! Contrary to "Jenks" report, they like the gearchange pattern and pointed out that, owing to the increased flexibility of the car, changing gear was not as necessary as on other 911 models.

16.7 mpg was all that *"Autocar"* were able to achieve from MYX 4L but they did admit that economy was not in any of the testers' minds when they drove the car!

When it came to the section headed "Handling, ride and brakes", the praise was high, but they still urged caution when approaching the roadholding limit and "slow in, fast out" was the method advised to take corners. They went on to caution that if the driver released the throttle when attempting a corner at too high a speed, the rear lost traction so suddenly that a spin was almost inevitable. Braking was adjudged "superb" with pedal effort neither too high nor too low whilst deceleration was measured at over 1G without any difficulty at all.

Summing up, *"Autocar"* said that besides being the fastest of a range of super sports cars, the Carrera RS was also the easiest to drive and the most exhilarating. They added the caution that it was a car needing more care than most high-performance cars but they thought it well worth that care.

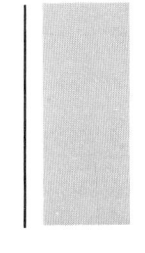

Original factory photos of the lightweight RS 2.7 litre Carrera.

Chapter 3

RSR

To achieve its aim to dominate the group 4 (special Grand Touring cars) class, Porsche took 48 of the 2.7 litre RSs from the assembly line and sent them to the competition department to have them converted to what they called "RSR" standard (Order no: M491). This involved taking off the normal ATE radially ventilated disc brakes and substituting the type 917 ventilated and drilled discs. Four-piston, copiously finned aluminium calipers operated on them front and rear. Twin master cylinders were used and a balance bar could alter the front/rear braking ratio.

9" front and 11" rear wheels were fitted with racing tyres of 230/600-15 and 260/600-15 sizes respectively. Titanium hubs utilizing magnesium wheels were available from the works. A wider than standard front air dam was fitted with the engine's oil cooler gathering its air through a slot in the centre. This bigger air dam brought its own problems. It turned what previously had been 35 kilogrammes of lift into 27 kilogrammes of downforce. Because, due to homologation requirements, the standard "Ducktail" spoiler only was allowed on the engine lid, this meant that rear end lift was now 57 kilogrammes and this made for a tendency to oversteer on fast bends, a less than desirable situation. This would not be cured until the advent of the 3-litre RSR.

Other features of the chassis were fasteners to hold down the front and engine covers. These were of glass reinforced plastic. A 24.2 gallon (110 litre) plastic fuel tank had its filler recessed into the plastic luggage compartment lid.

In the engine department more power was achieved by supplying new barrels of 92 mm bore thus bringing the capacity up to 2808 cc. Mahle racing pistons were employed and Carrera 6 camshafts were installed in new cam boxes with four bearings instead of the previous three to reduce bending stresses. The inlet and exhaust ports were opened up to 43 mm from the previous 38 mm and new, larger valves of 41.5 mm for the exhaust and 49 mm for the inlet were fitted. Twin-plug Marelli ignition made for better combustion and a smaller fan was installed. On a compression ratio of 10.5:1 308 bhp at 8,000 rpm resulted. Torque went up to 190 lb/ft at 5,100 rpm. This engine however, had an Achilles heel. Over long periods of racing time (in excess of 6 hours) the flywheel tended to work loose (they seemed to last out Le Mans, however!) A crankshaft damper was fitted which did help matters. On all RSRs, the plastic engine shroud was in plain coloured plastic which turned amber with heat.

A magnesium gearbox casing, as in the 2.7 RS, held the gears which were available to choice. A pump was used in the front cover of the casing and this was connected via pipes which led beneath the left-hand sill to an oil cooler or "Serpentine" which resided under the left front wheel arch. An 80% ZF or Getrag limited slip differential was fitted. A single plate clutch of similar dimensions to the 2.7 RS was fitted together with steel springs instead of rubber.

In addition, the Porsche badge on the front lid became a transfer, (lighter!) The ashtray and glovebox were omitted and there was no carpeting in the front compartment. The rear window was by Glaverbel and the passenger seat was omitted.

Porsche's sports department also altered the RS suspension to try to keep the racing tyres more in contact with the ground by shortening the diagonal rear suspension arms and moving their chassis mountings 15 mm outwards and 47.5 mm further back. Incidentally, this modification was also fitted to the last 181 2.7 RSs made.

At the front of the RSR, new suspension struts were fitted with the stub axle fitted 126 mm up the strut instead of 108 mm as standard. This enabled the front of the car to be lowered but still gave full suspension travel whilst not lowering the roll centre to an unacceptable degree. The rubber bushes in the normal suspension were replaced with delrin plastic bearings in the outer rear suspension arms and front wishbone pivots to give even better response to the steering. These give a characteristic "clonking" sound when the car is driven.

The factory, unlike previously where they had left the G.T. class to their private customers, ran two development cars in most of the 1973 races. One was mainly in group 4 whilst one was in the prototype class and developed as such. The stories of these two cars really fall outside the scope of this chapter and their adventures will be discussed in the chapter on the car's racing history.

The chassis numbers of the 48 2.8 litre RSR cars are:
386, 557, 601, 610, 614, 636, 643, 659, 701, 705, 714, 727, 755, 756, 760, 782, 784, 785, 791, 817, 837, 847, 853, 865, 871, 885, 894, 915, 921, 940, 960, 991, 997, 1008, 1033, 1045, 1054, 1088, 1099, 1113, 1134, 1155, 1159, 1183, 1196, 1329, 1497, 1521.

Amongst the notable first owners were the American, Peter Gregg, whose Brumos dealership took delivery of no less than five of these cars, chassis no: 727, 865, 940, 997 and 1113 whilst the Kremer Bros. cars were 0610 and 756. Claude Haldi drove chassis no: 659 whilst the Max Moritz cars were numbered 636 and 760. The George Loos car was numbered 847.

Paul Frere was, as far as we know, the only journalist to test a 2.8 litre RSR. He was invited to the racing department at Weissach at the end of every year to try their latest works car and we are grateful to the Porsche house magazine, *"Christophorous"* for their permission to reproduce the test.

On many occasions, the factory ran its works cars, always entered under the Martini banner, as prototypes, leaving to customers the task of defending the Porsche flag in the GT class. This was a good means of further developing the model for next year's GT races. In fact, even in their most advanced form, as they ran at Zeltweg in the 1000 km of Austria, the prototype Carreras differed very little from the GT version, even though the differences resulted in noticeably quicker lap times. The main differences were the wider wheels (11 in front and 14 in rear) with correspondingly wider wings, a considerably wider spoiler (with additional fins at Zeltweg) and lighter weight thanks to the use of plastic doors and a plastic front boot lid, perspex all-round (except, of course, for the windscreen), leaving out the spare wheel etc. The prototypes weighed in at around 890 kgs, some 40-50 kg less than the GT Carreras which, in racing trim, never got down to their homologation weight of 900 kg, mainly because there was never time enough to get down to the task of systematically lightening them.

Porsche's own test track, just outside their new Development Centre in Weissach, is extremely convenient for trying out any new development, both on the production and on the racing side. The original course, 3.1 km long, is called the mountain course and is full of very slow bends, most of them in "S" formation, plus a comparatively long straight and a medium fast 180° turn. It was designed at the time when Porsche were busy developing their ultra-lightweight cars for the European Mountain Championship in the years 1966-68. Around most of that course

Front view of the 1973 RSR. Note the front-mounted engine cooler

runs a rough track for chassis endurance testing, used for both production and racing development: all Porsche racing cars developed for long-distance racing do at least 1000 km on that track. Some of the tighter corners of the mountain course are by-passed by the 2.5 km long so-called "Can-Am" course which includes a fast, banked bend and is much faster than the mountain course. This is the more appropriate track for trying out the racing Carrera and this is where I was to take the wheel of the car that had been prepared for my visit.

Rear view of the RSR 2.8 (Order No M491)

R to RSR PORSCHE

The RS 2.7 and its racing development, the RSR 2.8 side by side at the factory

35

Needless to say, with all the controls in the same position as in the standard car and a perfectly dimensioned racing seat fully adjustable on the standard rails, I felt perfectly at home, stepping out of my own 911 S. Even the steering wheel is the standard size. I was informed that the rev limit was 8000 but that I should not worry overmuch, as there was an ignition cut-out coming into operation at 8200 rpm. As Porsche have been asked to reduce noise as much as possible, the car was fitted with expansion chambers attached to the tail pipes which, I was warned, caused some power loss – just how much I was later to find out.

The weather was dry, but cold and

for a few laps, before the D 38 Dunlop slicks had warmed up, the car felt rather skittish, but it gave me a chance to learn the Can-Am course on which I had never driven, taking it easy. It is not a course on which you can get away with too much exuberance, as some parts of the road are quite narrow and the wire fences pretty close. For a racing car, the lightness of the various controls is quite surprising. The racing clutch, which is reasonably progressive, is no heavier than that in my own car, thanks to the very cleverly

This is reputed to be the ex-Larrousse Tour de France RSR 2.8. Alex Marcoup drives it in 1974

arranged over centre helper spring which is now standard on all Porsches and braking too, which is not servo assisted (no Porsche ever had a servo) are no heavier than on the standard car. Higher gearing and wider racing tyres surely make steering heavier, but still quite reasonable, with quite excellent feel.

As tyres got warmer and myself more conversant with the circuit which is not particularly easy with a brow just on the apex of one bend and another bend hidden just behind another bump, the speed went up. Three bends I had been taking in second were now taken in third, though, obviously, the gearing was too high for the circuit, as in all three cases the car had to be accelerated out of the bend below 6000 rpm, which served to demonstrate the excellent flexibility of the engine which also proved to be very civilized when the car was driven back to base around the various buildings of the Research Centre.

The two humpback-like bumps showed up the pretty hard suspension but helped the car recover after jumping the one that is in the bend itself, with the back out of line. Handling was beautifully crisp, like a full-blood racing car, no doubt because of the

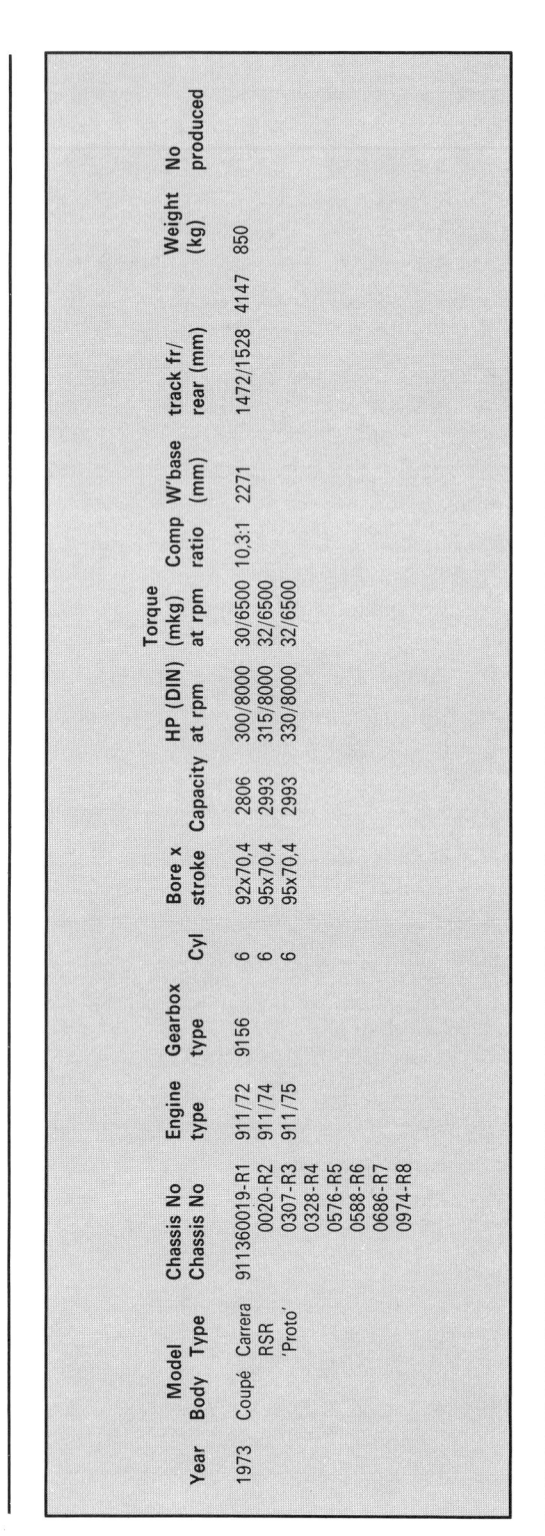

Year	Model Body Type	Chassis No Chassis No	Engine type	Gearbox type	Cyl	Bore x stroke	Capacity	HP (DIN) at rpm	Torque (mkg) at rpm	Comp ratio	W'base (mm)	track fr/ rear (mm)	Weight (kg)	No produced
1973	Coupé Carrera RSR 'Proto'	911360019-R1 0020-R2 0307-R3 0328-R4 0576-R5 0588-R6 0686-R7 0974-R8	911/72 911/74 911/75	9156	6 6 6	92x70,4 95x70,4 95x70,4	2806 2993 2993	300/8000 315/8000 330/8000	30/6500 32/6500 32/6500	10,3:1	2271	1472/1528	4147	850

elimination of all rubber in the suspension linkage and, in fact, the racing Carrera proved to be much easier to drive really fast than a standard Porsche, despite the notably higher limits: on the 190 m diameter steering pad in Weissach, the Carrera RSR is able to develop as much as 1.13 lateral g. For the prototype version with wider tyres and a larger spoiler 1.2 g is reached. For comparison, a standard Carrera on the best road tyres will reach 0.87 g, which is an extremely good performance for a road car.

One reason for the easier handling of the racing version is that its attitude is much less sensitive to the throttle opening, while there is never any doubt as to which end of the car will go first, for despite a feel of perfect steadiness in fast bends, the Carrera RSR will always oversteer at the limit and I felt that it could probably have been driven even faster if it had been more neutral and had made better use of the front wheel grip: "That is just the reason why we use even wider wheels and a larger rear spoiler when we run the Carrera as a prototype" was the answer Herr Singer, the engineer responsible for the Carrera racing project, gave me when I mentioned this to him.

The brakes were absolutely superb, which is not surprising when you remember they deal with nearly four times the power, more grip (thanks to much wider tyres and much more induced downthrust) and more weight (at least with the tanks full) in the CanAm car, but I felt the engine had surprisingly little urge at the top end. With the gearing used, I went into 5th at 7600 on the straight, as I felt there was very little to gain by staying in 4th until I had to brake for the 180° bend, which I could have done without exceeding the limit. "Well just do three or four laps with the silencers removed" said Development Chief Bott who had meanwhile turned up to watch the proceedings. The difference was quite startling. The engine now soared up to 8000, longing, it seems, for even more, and now I had to change up into 5th midway through the straight to prevent the rev counter needle from going into the red. There was also more noise in the car, but not to the point that one would have to drive with ear plugs.

The car I drove will eventually go into the Porsche museum. This seems rather a pity, but it has achieved its aim in providing the makers with useful lessons which will go into next year's GT racing models. Porsche think they can still learn from such participation, while such policy certainly points to the fact that despite all rumours of a front-engined car being developed in Zuffenhausen, the 911 series still has a bright future.

Chapter 4

RS 3 Litre

The 3-litre RS was what is now known as a "homologation special".

Reading the CSI rules, The Porsche racing management discovered that they need only build 100 examples of an "evolutionary" car to have the car included in Group 3 (Production G.T. Cars). Even the homologation documents supplied to the CSI by Porsche described the 3-litre RS as a "Face lift". In fact, the car was nearer to the 2.8 RSR than the 2.7 litre RS Carrera.

109 cars were built, Only 6 RHD cars being manufactured and 5 of these coming to Britain. One other car, chassis no: 9114609088 went to Japan. it was finished in red with gold "Carrera" side stripes. It is currently in Australia, coloured white. 57 of these 109 were converted to Group 4 RSR standard. The biggest single change from the RS 2.7 was actually in the materials used in the engine. To be more specific, the crankcase.

This had previously (since 1968) been made of AZ91 magnesium with the full race engine bored out to 95 mm. Apart from the problem of tending to shed its flywheel, this engine (as used in the factory development RSR) also tended to crack its crankcase due to the metal separating each bore becoming too thin and so a change to aluminium for more strength was instituted. Though this made for a weight penalty of 10 kilogrammes, the required strength was obtained.

Valve and port sizes were the same as before (2.7 litre engine) although the heads were different to accommodate the larger bore. The stud spacing became 83 mm, making the RS and RSR 3 litre a unique design as all subsequent production engines used an 86 mm stud spacing. The capacity now rose to 2994 cc, compression ratio was 9.8:1 and for once the car required 4-star fuel. Valve timing was standard "S" or Carrera. As in all 911s the crankshaft was a forging and had eight main bearings. Connecting rods were steel. The dry sump oil system featured a front mounted oil cooler as in the 2.8RSR aand the capacity of this system was 16 litres. Mechanical Bosch fuel injection was fitted as in the 2.7RS together with that

Head-on view as Nick Faure pilots 9114609100 to another victory in 1974

car's distributor whilst ignition was of the contact breaker less variety. Power output was 230 bhp at 6,200 rpm and torque was now 204 lb/ft at 5,000 rpm. The four-bearing camboxes and shafts were fitted.

The clutch had a reinforced diaphragm spring and the gearbox was similar to the 2.8 litre RSR together with its own pump and oil cooler. This took the shape of a "serpentine" of coiled piping and was fitted beneath the left front wheel arch. The naked pipes to this from the gearbox front cover were visible beneath the sill on that side. Gear ratios were: 3.182/1, 1.833/1, 1.261/1, 0.926/1 and 0.724/1. Reverse was 3.325/1 and the standard final drive was 4.429 whilst, once again, an 80% limited slip differential by ZF was fitted (part no: 901 332 05313).

Empty weight was given as 1985 lbs whilst front rims were 8" wide and the rears were 9" wide by 15" diameter. Tyres were Pirelli CN 36 of 215/60 VR15 and 235/60 VR15 size respectively.

Suspension of this RS model followed closely that of the 2.8 RSR in that the layout was the same with front torsion bars being 19 mm diameter with an

41

18 mm anti-roll bar. Rear torsion bars were 26 mm diameter also with 18 mm anti-roll bars. The semi-trailing arms at the rear were reinforced. Rear wheel bearings were larger than before. The front cross member was manufactured of steel. The rear suspension pick up points were as the 2.8 RSR. The front struts were the same as in 2.7 RS cars though the optional lowered front struts for racing could be fitted. For a road car the fitting of the 917 brake system with its ventilated and drilled discs of 300 mm was sensational. At the time, they cost as much as a small saloon car! (these had also been fitted to the 2.8 litre RSR.) The front compartment had a steel strut mounted between the front suspension towers to help strengthen the whole body structure.

Inside the cockpit, two Recaro bucket seats with reclining facility on the driver's side only were fitted and the rest of the interior was as in a 2.7RS lightweight, i.e. no rear seats, no clock and no glovebox lid and only one sun visor fitted. The cars were available in the usual Porsche range of colours with exterior window trim in black. Sound proofing was again minimal! To enable the RSR version of this car to fit 10.5" front and 14" rear wheel widths for racing, the 3-litre RS received much greater wheel arch width than before. It was of a size that would appear later on the production "Turbo", though the actual shape of the wheel arch was more rectangular on the RS. It was, in fact, a direct copy of the RSR 2.8.

Both front and rear bumper panels were made of glass reinforced plastic for lightness as were the front compartment lid and the rear engine cover. The front bumper panel now sported holes for cooling the front brakes as well as the opening for the front mounted oil cooler. The bodyshell itself, though appearing to be of 'G' road car specification was, in reality, the same as a 1973 RS 2.7 car. At the rear, a "Teatray" style of rear spoiler with a rubber surround was fitted. Lift was now down to 11 lbs at the front and 28.5 lbs at the rear at the car's theoretical maximum speed of 152 mph.

The actual performance of the car was not so different from a 2.7 RS in a straight line, the larger wheels, tyres and arches obviously creating more wind resistance but the roadholding and cornering forces were greatly increased. 0 to 100 mph took only 13.7 seconds whilst 0 to 60 mph was covered in 5.2 seconds. Service intervals were at an incredible 12,000 miles. The car was homologated in April 1974 in group 3 (production Grand touring cars). From the factory, the 3-litre RS cost DM 64,980 whilst the 5 right-hand drive cars that came to the U.K. cost £12,340.90p. The cars were built over the following period: July 1973 3 cars, August 6 cars,

Contrast. The difference between wheel arches and tyre widths can be seen here as an RSR and an RS 3.0 follow one another

RS 3.0 under rebuild displaying the oil piping to and from the engine and gearbox oil coolers

September 5 cars, October 2 cars, November 19 cars, December 16 cars, January 1974 21 cars, February 20 cars and, finally, in March of that year production ceased with 6 cars built.

The chassis numbers of the cars run from 9114609001 to 9114609109. Chassis

Head, cylinder, piston and rings from an RS during a rebuild

numbers of the cars which came to the U.K. are: 092, 097, 098, 099 and 100. In addition, left-hand drive cars in U.K. are: 018, 034 and 094. A list of chassis numbers and to whom they were first delivered follows.

Chassis Number	Engine Number	Production Number	Client
911 460 9020	684 0040	104 2099	Fa. Hahn, Stgt.
911 460 9018	684 0037	104 2100	Fa. Moritz, Reutlg.
911 460 9019	684 0038	104 2101	Fa. Raffay, Hamburg
911 460 9021	684 0039	104 2102	Fa. Glöckler, Ffm.
911 460 9022	684 0042	104 2103	Sonauto (Kd. Balsa)
911 460 9023	684 0043	104 2104	Fa. Raffay, Hamburg
911 460 9024	684 0052	104 2298	Fa. Schultz, Essen
911 460 9025	684 0048	104 2299	Presse
911 460 9026	684 0046	104 2300	Sonauto (Kd. Bonemaison)
911 460 9032	684 0051	104 2301	Sonauto
911 460 9029	684 0053	104 2302	–
911 460 9028	684 0044	104 2303	–
911 460 9030	684 0055	104 2551	–
911 460 9027	684 0047	104 2552	Amag, Schinznach-Bad
911 460 9031	684 0041	104 2553	–
911 460 9034	684 0061	104 2554	–
911 460 9044	684 0064	104 2555	–
911 460 9033	684 0049	104 2556	Porsche AG (H. Müller)
911 460 9035	684 0065	104 2767	(Wisdorf, Köln) Müller-Bräu
911 460 9036	684 0059	104 2769	–
911 460 9038	684 0045	104 2770	Hans Heuer
911 460 9037	684 0054	104 2771	–
911 460 9041	684 0058	104 2768	Fa. Moritz, Reutlg.
911 460 9039	684 0063	104 2766	Fa. Hahn, Stgt.
911 460 9042	684 0056	104 2987	–
911 460 9047	684 0057	104 2988	Bosshardt (Amag)
911 460 9043	684 0062	104 2989	–
911 460 9045	684 0050	104 2990	–
911 460 9046	684 0060	104 2991	Smorawinsky
911 460 9079	684 0119	104 4364	Mahag, München (H. Haberl)
911 460 9081	684 0120	104 4365	Hofer
911 460 9082	684 0107	104 4366	Amag (Kd. Bordilatz)
911 460 9084	684 0110	104 4566	Amag
911 460 9085	684 0105	104 4567	Hertel
911 460 9084	684 0115	104 4568	H. Blind, (Hahn)

44

911 460 9090	684 0104	104 4569	Greger, Dachau
911 460 9088	684 0109	104 4570	Japan
911 460 9096	684 0117	104 4571	Fa. Schultz (Kd. Birkner)
911 460 9091	684 0111	104 4887	Schickentanz
911 460 9093	684 0112	104 4888	H. Thomas (Zbinden)
911 460 9094	684 0113	104 4889	Amag (Kd. v. Karajan)
911 460 9092	684 0118	104 4892	AFN
911 460 9103	684 0106	104 4891	Hamilton
911 460 9097	684 0116	104 4897	AFN
911 460 9098	684 0114	104 4898	AFN
911 460 9099	684 0108	104 4899	AFN
911 460 9100	684 0103	104 4900	AFN
911 460 9105	684 0123	104 6342	Strapason
911 460 9106	684 0124	104 6343	Vorführwagon
911 460 9108	684 0121	104 6344	Keller
911 460 9107	684 0122	104 6379	R. Mey
911 460 9109	684 0125	104 6492	Klein

This right-hand drive RS 3.0 was first owned by James Hunt. With only 14,000 miles on the clock it belongs today to a private collector

R to RSR PORSCHE

Very few road tests were conducted of the 3.0 RS but Paul Frere reported on the German demonstrator car, (registration no S-AY 2511) in both *"Motor"* and *"Road and Track"*. After describing the car, Frere went on to say that on a value-for-money basis, the driver interested in fast road work was actually better off buying the previous year's 2.7 litre RS!

Frere recorded acceleration times of 5.2 seconds and 13.7 seconds for the 0 to 60 and 0 to 100 mph marks respectively with a top speed of 149 mph. On his way to the Casala track near Turin, Frere averaged 124 mph over 78 miles of Autostrada, despite being held up by a lorry in road works over two miles. One wonders what the speed would have been without this temporary hold up!

At the track, Paul Frere found that fast bends needed to be approached with some power on, whilst getting around the bend still required some delicacy. On tight or hairpin bends, the car tended to understeer due to its 80% limited slip differential and required the tail swinging around under power. Back on the road, he noticed that the wide tyres and stiff anti-roll bars tended to make the car follow road irregularities but that wind noise was low and that he suffered no more fatigue than in his own 911S.

To conclude, Paul Frere commented on the 12,000 mile service intervals of the car and pointed out that there was

Nick Faure demonstrates the meaning of the word 'oversteer'! Whilst the Lotus Elan demonstrates understeer!

no doubt that the car would go on and on delivering its massive performance with the utmost reliability and needing no more than routine attention.

John Anderton, of AFN the British distributor, invited Roger Bell, the editor of *"Motor"* to sample their demonstrator, VVB 3M over a weekend.

Bell commented in the report that this Carrera replaced the Ferrari 275 GTB/4 as the car he would most like to own and that he received complaints from his passengers about their suffering neck muscles under full-throttle acceleration and heavy braking. Of the latter, the reporter said that the car must have achieved over 1G from 100 mph whilst he was testing the car on slicks at the Castle Combe circuit. With these racing tyres fitted, the car's ride became much harder and the steering even more responsive but Bell found it difficult to find the cornering limits of the car without visiting the scenery! Nick Faure, who was winning Modsports races that year with almost monotonous regularity said that when the Porsche got really out of shape in a corner, he simply let go of the wheel and let the car sort itself out!

For *"Sports Car World"*, October 1974, Jerry Sloniger reported on testing the German demonstrator, the same car that Paul Frere had tested, over 1,000 kilometres. Sloniger said that he only cursed occasionally, when he was baulked by slower cars and when he had to pay for another tankful of 4-star fuel.

At Hockenheim, the demonstrator, now with over 12,000 miles on the clock, stubbornly refused to raise its oil temperature above 80 degrees Centigrade and indicated 70-75 lbs/sq. in. oil pressure. He reported the same handling traits as had Frere, while commenting that even when he entered one bend just too fast, the Carrera stayed with him and they finished up pointing in the right direction.

Jerry Sloniger concluded by writing that the Porsche 3.0 RS was incredibly easy to drive at eight or nine tenths and very much a tightrope act after that. He said that 135 mph came up quickly but the remaining 14 mph seemed to take forever. Final comment was by Dr. Fuhrmann who said that he liked a car with "a reserve of power". This Porsche, said Sloniger, has got it.

"Motoring News", in their August 8th, 1974 edition, were lucky to be able to borrow Jack Tordhoff's RS 3.0 with its personalised registration number, JCT 600. In the week that ensued, the writers of the article were able to report that the car's behaviour in traffic was "as docile as a kitten" until they put their foot down. The RS then became "a real beast of a car" as one passenger said. They also commented on the fact that the car owed little heritage to any road-going machinery and that it was simply a road-going racing car.

After describing the car mechanically, the reporters said that the engine was slightly off-song and they didn't try for maximum revs in fifth but the RS still recorded 0 to 60 mph in 5.3 seconds.

"Motoring News" stated the homologation weight to be 17.7 cwt, thus giving a power to weight ratio of 260 bhp per ton. They went on to describe fast, open bends as "a real joy", finding themselves thinking they were doing 90 mph and looking at the speedometer to find

A standard 911S which has received an RS 2.7 air dam

The 1972 Kremer prepared 911S 2.5 driven by John Fitzpatrick to win the 1972 European G.T. Championship

R to RSR PORSCHE

Another lovely restoration of an RS 2.7 Carrera 'lightweight'

Michael Burt at Snetterton in March 1986 in the 'Giroflex' race with his RS 2.7 Carrera

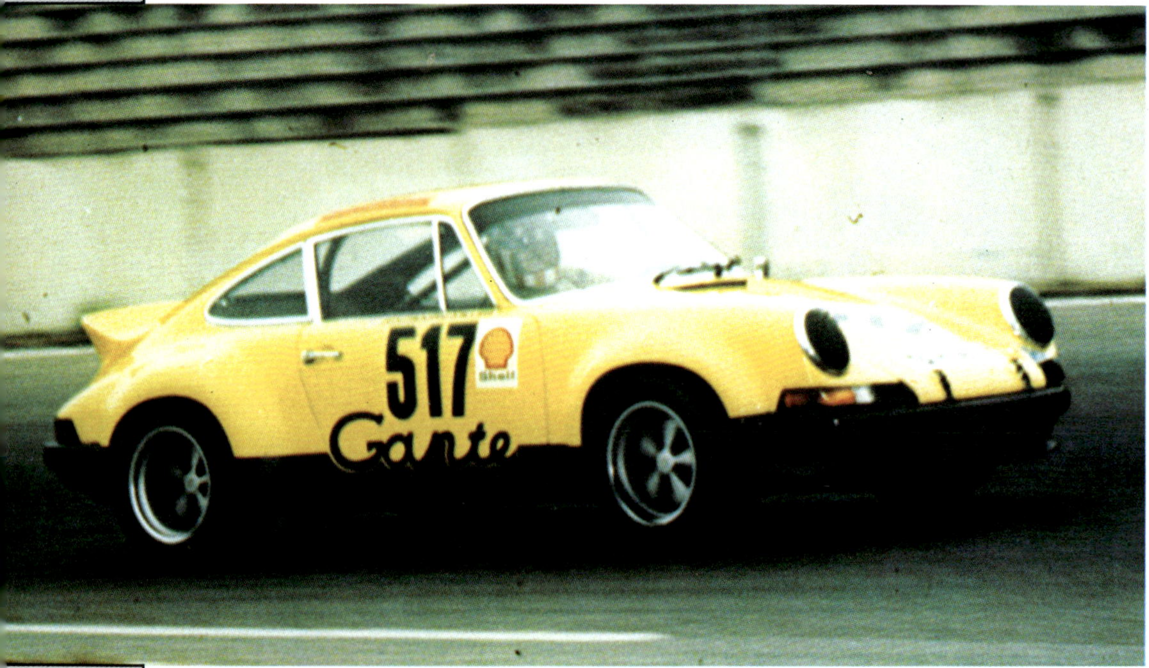
517
Shell
Garte

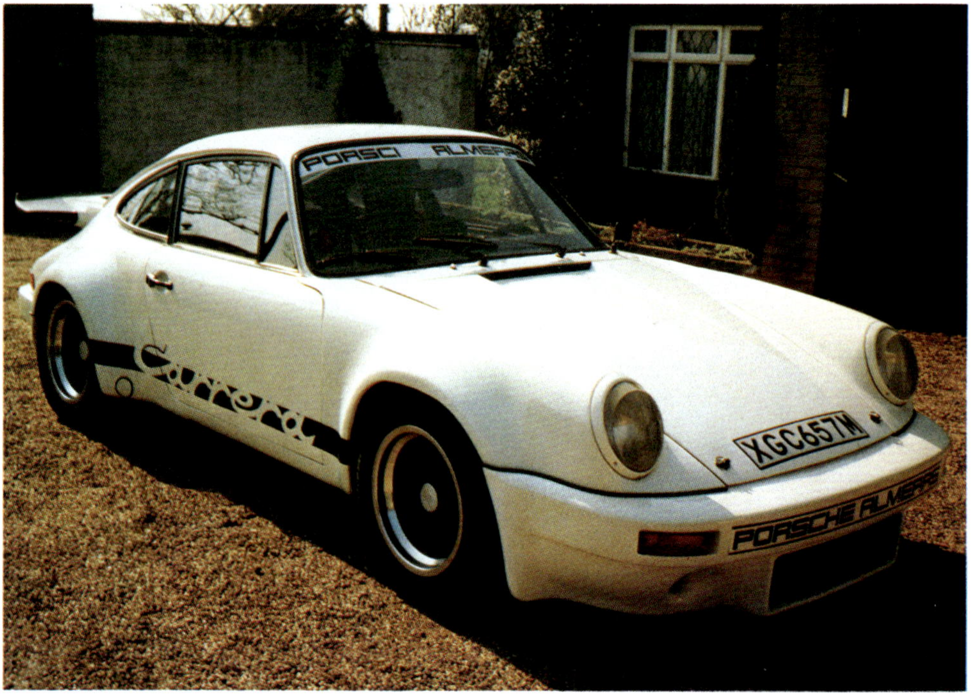
PORSCHE ALMERAS
XGC657M

Top left: The RSR 2.8 litre of Jay Rulon-Miller practising in 1973

Bottom left: Author's pride! RS 3.0 chassis no. 9114609034, G.T. winner Le Mans 1976 – now fully restored

Above: The AFN demonstrator RS 3.0 today, chassis no. 9114609100 ex-Nick Faure Modsports winner and Irish Rally car

Right: RS 3.0 which was originally an RS 2.7 The car was re-shelled at the factory after a crash and updated

R to RSR PORSCHE

Top: The exposed gear cluster of an RS 3.0 in its casing
Above: Cam box from an RS 3.0 engine
Inset: One of the five RS 3.0 right-hand drive cars imported into Great Britain in 1974

Violent Vaillant! The lurid colour scheme of 9115609117 brightens up a winter's day in Cologne

R to RSR PORSCHE

The air intake slot to the rear brakes of an RSR 3.0

Interior of RSR 3.0. Note the 10,000 rpm tachometer and lack of clock and speedometer

the RS doing 120 mph!

On tight corners they reported a different story, being unable to make the back slide, this probably being due to the limited slip differential as well as the width of rubber but of the stopping ability of the 917 type brakes they had no doubt.

"Motoring News" came to the conclusion that the RS 3.0 had only one true home and that was on a race track or in tarmac rallies. What a shame, they said, to just use this car to burn up the by-pass. Their final paragraph stated that one week with the RS 3.0 had been "the motoring experience of a lifetime!"

Group 3
General Data:
Dimensions:
Length	166.8 in
Width	70.0 in
Height	52.0 in

Track:
front	56.6 in
rear	57.6 in

Empty weight:
1984 lbs	(homologation)

Performance:
0-100 km (62 mph)	5.3s
0-200 km (124 mph)	21.1s
1/4 mile, standing start	13.7 s
500 m (547 yds)	15.8 s
1000 m (1094 yds)	25.0 s
Top speed	152 mph

Tyres and Rims:
Front
Pirelli CN 36	215/60 VR 15

on 8" Fuchs rims
Rear
Pirelli CN 36	235/60 VR 15

on 9" Fuchs rims
Spacers for front and rear axles
Thickness	front 0.28 in
	rear 1.18 in

Engine:
Model 911/77
Cylinders	6
Bore $\varnothing$	95.0 mm
Stroke	70.4 mm
Capacity	2992.55 cc
Capacity per cylinder	498.76 cc
Compression	9.8:1
Output	230 hp at 6200 rpm
Max. torque	202.5 lbs-ft at 5000 rpm
Specific output	76.6 hp/litre
Fuel	Super (98 octane)

Engine design:
Type	Four-stroke Otto engine (opposed)
Cooling	Air
Fan drive	Belt
Crankcase	Light metal
Crankshaft	Forged, plain bearings
Connecting rods	Forged steel, plain bearings
Pistons	Light metal
Cylinders	Individual, light metal
Cylinder heads	Single-cylinder, light metal
Valves	1 intake, 1 exhaust per cylinder
Valve $\varnothing$	Intake $\varnothing$ 1.93 in Exhaust $\varnothing$ 1.63 in

Valve springs	2 coil springs per valve
Valve drive	1 overhead camshaft per cylinder bank with rocker arms
Camshaft drive	2 dual chains
Lubrication	Dry sump with oil tank and 1 oil filter
Oil cooling	1 cooler in nose
Oil capacity	16.8 qt
Intake system	1 throttle valve housing per cylinder bank, 1 triple intake tube per bank, air filter system, twin-row injection pump, toothed belt drive
Exhaust system	With muffler
Electrics	Bosch single ignition as in production cars

Gearbox
5-speed gearbox with splash lubrication and oil pump, oil cooling via cooling tube in left front wheel arch
Oil capacity   4 qt
Limited slip differential with 80% locking factor
Gearbox and axle ratios as in Series G-programme, interchangeable

Clutch
Fichtel & Sachs
Production clutch with 1875-2050 lb force
(Pressure plate from 2.8 litre racing Carrera)
Clutch pedal with over-centre spring

Bodywork
Frame:
Sheet metal parts
Roof skin
Door outer skin
Seat tubs
Shift console

Strengthening and braces
Spring leg bearing strengthened
Rear stabilizer bearing strengthened
Driver's foot rest
Cross member rear and front track altered, to allow installation of coil springs

FRP Parts:
Front bumper with integral oil cooler casing
Rear bumper
Trunk lid with standard lock
Rear spoiler lid with rubber edge and standard lock
(Racing spoiler lid provided)

Fenders:
Steel, front extended for 9" wheels
Rear extended for 11" wheels

Glazing:
Windshield, standard laminated glass of 0.16"
Thin glass sides and rear
Rear window fixed

Paint:
Grand Prix White

Interior fittings:
Largely identical to RSR 1973

black felt, simple door panels without lock moulding door release by thong

Drivers seat: Recaro lightweight, adjustable back

Co-driver seat: Recaro racer (seats interchangeable for track use)

4 point safety belts

Dash as in Series G911 Carrera without clock (hole covered by fibreglass lid)

Black head liner

Without roll bar or cage but arrangement for mounting
Without main battery switch

General:
Window frames and exterior mirror matt black and headlamp rings in car colour. Body without sound-proof mats and only partially sprayed with Tectyl L undercoating.

Trunk lid without gas-filled stays, held by catches. Fuel tank Series G programme. Spare wheel with 6" Fuchs rims (165-15 tyre)

Chassis
The chassis largely corresponds to the '73 RSR

Front axle:
Aluminium carriers
Strengthened arms
Bilstein shock legs, adjustable as in Carrera RS 2.7 (but stronger version)
Standard arm bearings

Steering:
Standard steering: raised
Zero track

Front springing:
Torsion bar 0.75$\varnothing$
Stabilizer 0.71", not adjustable

Rear axle:
Short steel arms strengthened, swivel bearings
Adjustable Bilstein shock absorbers as in Carrera RS 2.7

Springing:
Torsion bar 1.02"$\varnothing$
Stabilizer 0.71", not adjustable
Standard spring strut bearings

Brakes:
917 brake system with Porsche brake saddles, transversely ribbed (Axially and radially ventilated brake discs, 4-piston saddles)

Piston $\varnothing$ front	1.69 in
rear	1.50 in
2 main brake cylinders	front 0.67 in rear 0.87 in

Balance-beam adjustment for brake balance
Handbrake – drum for rear wheels

Chapter 5

RSR 3.0

The 3-litre RSR was Porsche's final normally aspirated racing car. So successful was it that, apart from winning all the world G.T. championships it was entered for, even today it can still win any race for which it is eligible on the club scene if it were not for the fact that the majority of them have become collector's pride and joys or languish in museums.

Using the 3-litre RS as a base, the 57 cars taken from the "production line" were sent to the competition department and altered as follows:

An extra 12 mm plug hole was bored in the cylinder heads to take the twin ignition system which had also been a feature of the 2.8 litre car. Valve lift of the cams now went up to 12.2 mm (from 12.1 mm) for the inlet and 11.5 mm (from 10.6 mm) for the exhaust. The timing was the same as before.

The fuel injection pump was uprated for greater flow whilst it was found necessary to employ slide throttles instead of the more normal butterfly type to bring the power up to 330 bhp at 8,000 rpm. With the butterfly throttles, only 308 bhp had resulted. The torque was now 232 lb/ft. A "straight through" exhaust system was employed resulting in two tail pipes at the rear.

The gearbox was as for the RS 3.0 litre with oil cooler and pump and final drive was 7/37 or 7/31. Numerous gear ratios were available for tailoring the car to different circuits. Zandvoort circuit in Holland was set up using 7/37 rear axle ratio with a 28/24 fifth gear whilst the Mainz-Fruthen airport circuit demanded a 7/31 final drive ratio and a 26/26 fifth gear speed to give a maximum speed of 186 kph.

A Fichtel and Sachs single plate clutch was employed, lined with sintered metal to cope with the extra power. For the suspension, the front struts had the stub axles raised by 18 mm in order to lower the front of the car and retain its suspension travel, whilst the rear suspension was as the 3-litre RS with its modified pick-up points.

Titanium or steel coil springs could now be fitted as auxiliary springing for the track whilst light alloy dampers went with the titanium springs. The front

The Asa Cachia RSR 3.0 raced several times at Le Mans. Note the screen washers!

camber was now set at 1 degree 20' negative whilst at the rear it became 25' negative. The castor was 6 degrees 30' whilst there was 25' toe in at the rear and none at the front.

Wheels were now 10.5" front and 14" at the rear sporting slicks of 245/575-15" (front) and 305/575-15" (rear). For wet conditions, the factory recommended 9" front and 12" rear wheel sizes. Centre-locking was used to secure the wheels to the axles and to facilitate rapid wheel changes. To cover these wide wheels and tyres the wings were enlarged the 2" allowed by the rules but now employed a new shape whereby the front wings ended abruptly in front of the doors and allowed the hot air from the brakes to exit via slots covered with wire mesh. Behind the doors, similar slots were cut into the front and rear of the rear wing extensions to serve the same purpose for the rear brakes.

The rest of the bodywork was very similar to the RS version except that a larger rear spoiler was fitted which overhung the rear bumper. This was fitted with an auxiliary grille to extract hot air from the engine compartment.

Lift forces at the front were 103 lbs, at the rear, 83 lbs, both these figures calculated at 152 mph. Weight was between 925 and 950 kilogrammes for customer versions. A special Recaro seat with high squab and headrest was fitted for the driver, there being no passenger seat whilst a six-point seatbelt was fitted together with a fire extinguisher system and a flexible safety fuel tank containing 24.2 Imp. gallons feeding through twin fuel pumps. A 10,000 rpm tachometer was fitted. The gearbox was as in the RS version, complete with oil cooler, whilst a large variety of ratios could be chosen.

Brakes were as the RS version, i.e. 917 type, but wider calipers to take wider brakepads for long distance races could be specified at the front.

Chassis numbers were: 9114609040 (a car used for development) followed by nos. 9114609048 to 9114609078 inclusive followed by singleton examples of 9080, 9083, 9086, 9087 and 9095.

We have also come across 2 RSRs

RSR 3.0 belonging to Peter Lovett, now fully restored

Facia of an RSR. This one even sports a clock

The central locking of an RSR wheel. Photo also shows 'helper' coil spring and massive 917 brakes

R to RSR PORSCHE

The underside of 9115609121 showing the exhaust brace and central jacking point

numbered 9115609017 and 9121 suggesting that further cars were built for the 1975 season. The factory can find records of building 9121, 9122 and 9123 but it would seem reasonable to presume that the "56" chassis numbers were carried on from 9114609109 thus giving another batch of fourteen RSRs built.

And so we come to the end of the line for the RS and RSR cars. The factory was already looking forward to 1976 with the new rules looming and had already been seen using a 2.14 litre engine fitted with a turbocharger. Although the RSRs could not compete with this car in terms of sheer power, their light weight and tremendous throttle response has kept them a favourite ever since.

Erwin Kremer (plus rabbit!) waits at the side of 9115609117 in a paddock in Europe in 1975

Group 4 Racing Version

Alterations to Group 3:

Tyres and rims
Front:
9" magnesium alloy rims in spoke fork (like 917) with
Rain tyres
Dunlop 230/600-15 CR 88 D 15 356"
Rear:
12" magnesium alloy rims in spoke form (like 917) with
Rain tyres
Dunlop 260/600-15 CR 88 D 15 356"

Special order rims:

Front:
$10^{1}/_{2}$" magnesium alloy rims (spoke form)

Rear:
14" magnesium alloy rims (spoke form)

For these rims the customer must provide the proper racing tyres (slicks). Slicks are not delivered by Porsche AG.

Engine
Model 911/75

Cylinders	6
Bore	95 mm
Stroke	70.4 mm
Capacity	2992.55 cc
Compression	10.3:1
Output	330 hp at 8000 rpm
Max. torque	231.5 lbs-ft at 6500 rpm
Specific output	110 hp/litre

Engine design:

Type	Four-stroke Otto engine (opposed)
Cooling	Air
Fan drive	Belt
Crankcase	Light metal
Crankshaft	Forged, plain bearings
Connecting rods	Forged steel, plain bearings
Pistons	Light metal
Cylinders	Individual, light metal
Oil cooling	1 cooler in nose
Intake system	1 throttle slide per cylinder bank

PORSCHE

	1 intake throat per cylinder head Twin-row injection pump, toothed belt drive
Exhaust system	1 individual-tube system per bank with collector and diffuser
Electrics	Bosch twin ignition with contactless distributor and adjustable electronic rev limiter

Clutch

Racing clutch from Fichtel & Sachs
Single-plate dry clutch with increased pressure
Clutch disc with spring torsional damper and racing lining (Kerasinter)

One of the three 1975 RSR 3.0 run by the Kremer brothers for the European G.T. Championship

Charles Ivey attends to the engine of Jay Rulon-Miller's RSR 3.0 in the paddock at Le Mans. Note the oil cooler pipes running from the front of the gearbox

Bodywork

Fender extensions of FRP (fibre-reinforced polyester)
Front and rear bumpers attuned to fender extensions
Recaro racing seat with slots for 6-point safety belt, 3″ wide
Tachometer reading of 10,000 rpm

Fire extinguisher system from Heinzmann
Roll bar

Cylinder heads	single-cylinder, light metal
Valves	1 intake, 1 exhaust per cylinder

Valve	Intake 1.93 in
	Exhaust 1.63 in
Valve springs	2 coil springs per valve
Valve drive	1 overhead camshaft per cylinder bank with rocker arms
Camshaft drive	2 dual chains
Lubrication	Dry sump with oil tank and 2 oil filters
Tank	29 gallon plastic tank
	2 fuel pumps

Chassis:

Front wheel arms
Precision bearings, Delrin bushings
Rear axle arms:
Precision bearings, Delrin bushings
Hubs:
Centre-lock
Rims:
Magnesium alloy in spoke form like 917
Front axle
9" (Rain tyres)
Rear axle
12" (Rain tyres)
Brakes:
Thermodynamically improved front brakes for long-distance racing.
Shock absorbers:
Bilstein V8/H8
With threads for coil spring installation
Special order:
Coil springs front and rear in steel

The rear suspension arm of an RSR 3.0

The body parts necessary for an RSR 3.0. In the background is one of the Kremer cars

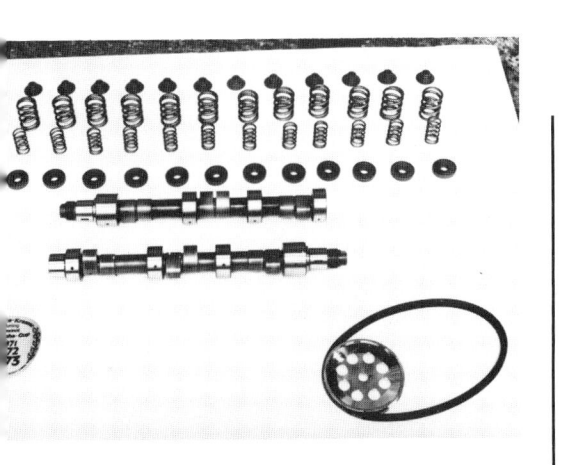

The Schrick developed 4-bearing camshafts used on the 1975 Kremer RSRs. With these installed power was up to 345 bhp

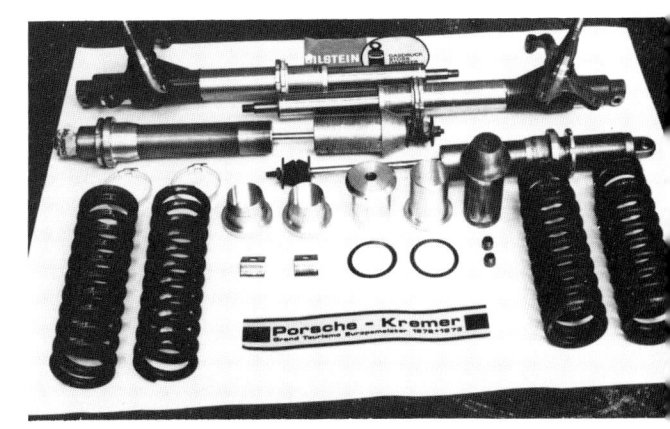

The Bilstein dampers, front stubs and titanium springs used on the Kremer-prepared 1974-1975 RSR 3.0 cars

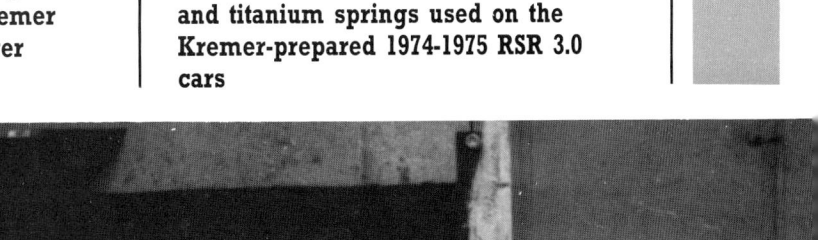

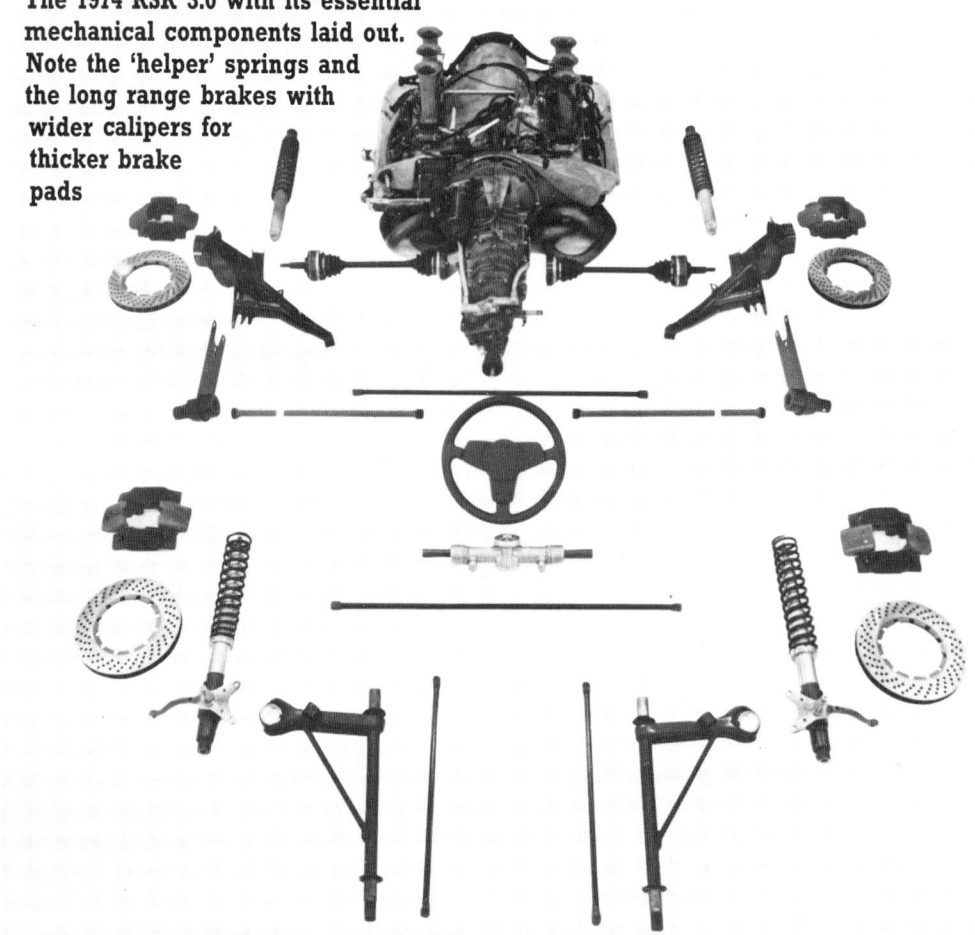

The 1974 RSR 3.0 with its essential mechanical components laid out. Note the 'helper' springs and the long range brakes with wider calipers for thicker brake pads

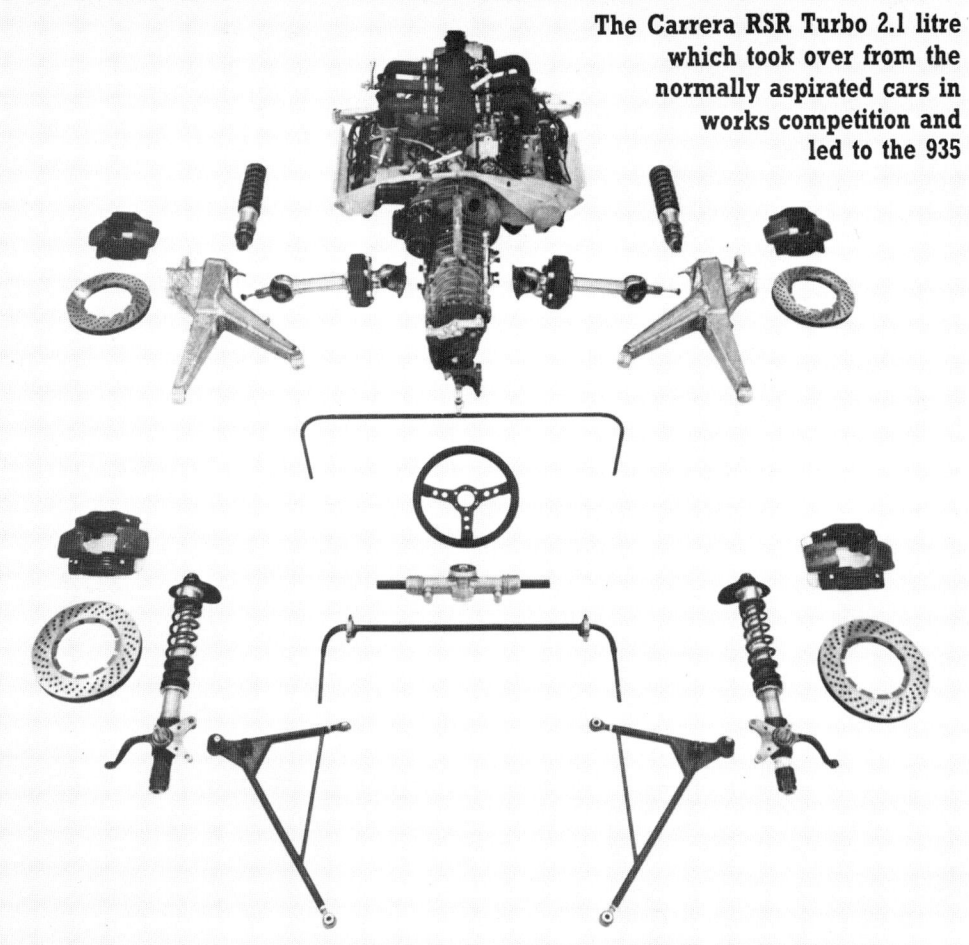

The Carrera RSR Turbo 2.1 litre
which took over from the
normally aspirated cars in
works competition and
led to the 935

Carrera 2.7 RS/2.8 RSR/3.0 RS/3.0 RSR

Year	Body	Model Type	Chassis No	Engine type	Gearbox type	Cyl	Bore x stroke	Capacity	HP (DIN) at rpm	Torque (mkg) at rpm	Comp ratio	W'base (mm)	Track fr rear (mm)	Length (mm)	Weight (kg)	No produced
1973	Coupé	Carrera 2.7	9113600288/285	911/83	915	6	90x70.4	2687	210/6300	26/5100	8.5:1	2271	1372/1394	4147	980	2
1973	Coupé	Carrera 2.7 Safari														
		Carrera 2.8 RSR	9113600386-1549	911/72	915	6	92x70.4	2806	300/8000	30/6500	10.3:1	2271	1402/1421	4147	900	49
1974	Coupé	Carrera 3.0 RS	9114609001-9109	911/77	915	6	95x70.4	2993	230.6200	28/5000	9.8:1	2271	1437/1462	4235	900	109 PLUS
1974	Coupé	Carrera 3.0 RSR	9114609001-9109	911/74 911/75	915	6 6	95x70.4 95x70.4	2993 2993	315/8000 330/8000	32/6500 32/6500	10.3:1 10.3:1	2271	1472/1528	4235	920	109 PLUS

	911 2.4/2.7	Carrera 2.7 RS	2.8 RSR	Carrera 2.7	2.7 Safari	3.0 RS	3.0 RSR
Engine							
Crankcase	Magnesium	As 911	As 911	As 911	As 911	Aluminium	Aluminium
Crankshaft	Stroke 70.4	As 911	As 911	As 911	As 911	As 911	As 911
Con rod	Steel	As 911	As 911	As 911	As 911	As 911	As 911, 2.0, Titanium
Camshaft	3 bearings	As 911	Modified timing and lift, 4 bearings	As 911	As 911	As 911	Modified timing and lift, 4 bearings
Valves	46/40 Ø	As 911	As 911	As 911	As 911	Larger Ø	As 3.0 RS
Injection	2.4 mech	Mechanical	Mechanical	Mechanical	Mechanical	Mechanical	Mechanical
Ignition	2.7 K Jetronic Single with breaker	As 911	Twin with breaker	As 911	As 911	As 911	Twin, no breaker
Cooling blower	11 blades	As 911	Ø smaller	As 911	As 911	As 911	As 2.8 RSR
Oil Cooler	—	Serpentine	Front	Serpentine	Serpentine	Front	Front

Running gear						
Front axle	MacPherson	As 911	As 911	As 911	As 911	As 911
Rear axle	Semi-trailing arms	As 911	As 911	As 911	As 911	As 2.8 RSR
Pivot	Rubber	As 911	As 911	As 911	As 911	Delrin/Unibal
Springs, front	Torsion bar 19 Ø	As 911	Delrin/Unibal As 911 + auxil spring	As 911	As 911	As 911 + auxil spring
Springs, rear	Torsion bar 23 Ø	As 911	Torsion bar 26 Ø + auxil spring	As 911	Torsion bar 26 Ø	As 2.8 RSR + auxil spring
Dampers	Hydraulic, double acting	As 911, different setting	As 911, different setting	As 911	As 2.7 RS	As 2.8 RSR
Brakes, front	Cast-iron caliper 911	Aluminium caliper 911	917 short distance	As 911	As 2.8 RSR	917 long distance
Brakes, rear	Cast-iron caliper 911	As 911	917 short distance	As 911	As 2.8 RSR	917 long distance
Ventilated brake discs	Plain	As 911	Perforated	As 911	Perforated	Perforated
Rim width	6"/6"	6"/7"	9"/11"	6"/7"	5½" f M + S tyres 8"/9"	10½"/14"
Clutch						
Diameter (mm)	225	As 911	As 911	As 911	As 911	As 911
Lining	Organis	As 911	As 911	As 911	Sintered metal	Sintered metal
Damper	Rubber	As 911	Steel spring	As 911	Steel spring	Steel spring
Spring pressure	Standard	Higher	Higher	As 2.7 RS	As 2.8 RSR	Higher
Gearbox						
Housing	Magnesium	As 911	As 911	As 911	As 911	As 911
Jet lubrication + cooler	–	–	Yes	–	Yes	Yes
Lim slip diff	Optional	As 911	80%	As 911	40%	80%
Half shafts	Constant velocity	As 911	As 911	As 911	As 911	As 911
Gear selector	Aluminium	As 911	As 911	As 911	As 911	As 911
Body						
Wheel arches, width	Standard	Rear widened	Front and rear widened	As 2.7 RS	As 2.8 RSR	Plastic extensions front and rear
Rear spoiler	–	Duck's tail	Duck's tail	Tray spoiler opt	Duck's tail	Tray spoiler
Interior trim	Standard	Simplified	Spartan	De luxe	Simplified	Spartan
Weight (without fuel)	1025 kg	900 kg	917 kg	1037 kg	1000 kg	800 kg	817 kg

Chapter 6
Racing in Europe

Because of the sheer amount of racing done in 911s, both by the works and in the hands of private owners, we have found it simpler to split Europe and America into separate chapters. Therefore, in this chapter we are going to be looking at the cars' (and drivers') careers in Europe. This really started with Eberhard Mahle winning the G.T. class of the European Hillclimb Championship in 1966.

At that most famous and prestigious of endurance races, Le Mans, the 911 made its first appearance. Strictly speaking, as a relatively standard car, it doesn't have a place in this book but as next year saw four 911s entered, we thought it should be included.

Anyway, this particular car, entered by Jacques Dewez, was driven by Kerguen and "Franc". It came 14th overall and 12th in the index of performance. It won the 2-litre GT class and was only beaten in the overall G.T. class by a Ferrari 275 GTB. It was driven to the track for the event and, afterwards, driven home.

Once the 911S had been homologated in 1967, Porsche lost no time in getting it into the hands of various owners and in May at the Nurburgring 1000 kilometres Helmutt Kelleners/Jurgen Neuhaus were placed 11th overall and 1st in the 2-litre G.T. class whilst Sepp Gregor/Multe Huth were 12th overall and 2nd in the 2-litre G.T. class.

Come Targa Florio time and Jean-Claude Killy/Bernard Cahier came 7th overall and once again took the class G.T. win. At Le Mans this time, four 911Ss were entered, though only one finished and this in 14th place, again being beaten by a Ferrari 275 GTB. The drivers were Buchet and Linge.

Jean-Pierre Gabin and "Pedro" took a 911S to Spa for the production car 24 hour race and won. By this time, halfway through the season, the 911R came on stream and one was run by the works, equipped with the new "Sportomatic" transmissions. It was driven by Vic Elford/Hans Hermann/Jochen Neerpasch in the Marathon de la Route, an 84 hour "trial" at the Nurburgring. The factory also entered two other cars. One a 911S, again with "sportomatic"

4-speed gearbox and another 911S with a standard 5-speed manual gearbox. The "R", crewed by Elford/Hermann/Neerpasch won the event with a clear 34 laps over the second placed car, an MGC. The other two cars did not finish, one falling out with valve problems whilst the other crashed.

The 911R was also involved, this time in manual gearbox form in a session of record taking at Monza. This came about because a 906 being run for the same purpose by Rico Steinemann, Dieter Spoerry, Jo Bonnier and Charles Vogele had broken its dampers whilst attempting the same records. Steinemann phoned the factory and Dr. Helmutt Bott who was then in charge of chassis development agreed. It was pointed out to him that 5th gear was not expected to stand up to the 20,000 kilometres run to be attempted and so the solution was to give the "R" two fifth gears! (another 5th instead of 4th gear) The engine used turned out to have already done a 100 hour endurance test on the Dynamometer but it still managed to stand up splendidly to the attempt, taking five world and fourteen 2-litre class records up to 20,000 kilometres. In fact, of the world records taken, only 0.66 of a mile per hour separated the slowest from the fastest (130.67 mph). The European Group 3 Hillclimb championship, meanwhile, had been taken by Toni Fischaber.

By 1968 the 911 had been allowed to enter the British saloon car championship and Vic Elford won the 2-litre class at the Race of Champions meeting and followed this with victory at Silverstone. Toine Hezemans came over from Holland to take a class 2nd in the Motor Show 200 mile race held at Brands Hatch. Elford also led the Snetterton 500 kilometre race in April but retired after covering 21 laps when a rocker broke.

At the Nurburgring 1,000 kilometres in May, Greger and Huth won the group 3 class as well as coming 18th overall. They were the 2nd G.T. car home after the G.T. 40 driven by Mike Salmon and David Piper. Group 3 was also dominated by a 911T at the Monza 1,000 kilometres later that May with Dieter Glemser and Hugo Kelleners driving the class winner. At the Targa Florio, Claude Haldi/Greub came as high as 8th overall in a field dominated by prototypes.

Le Mans this year was held in September rather than May due to the political unrest in France and a 911S driven by Gaban/Vanderschriek came 12th overall, thus winning the G.T. class and averaging 97.96 mph. Four 911s were entered, two finished and two retired including a personal disappointment for the one driven by Claude Ballot-Lena/Chasseuil whose engine expired a mere two laps from the end.

After their group 3 victory at Monza, Glemser and Kelleners did it again at the Spa event over a similar distance, this time finishing 11th overall whilst in the Spa 24 hour production car race, Erwin Kremer and Willy Kauhsen took top honours, winning outright with the three other 911s entered finishing in the first ten.

The Marathon de la Route, that 84-hour thrash around the Nurburgring, was won this time by Linge/Glemser and Kauhsen driving what was purported to be a 911E but which was in fact an "S" fitted wth Boge self-levelling struts.

The Hezemans/Fitzpatrick RSR at Dîjon in April 1975. This car won the G.T. class

A scene typical of Porsche club racing today. Michael Burt puts the power on exiting a corner at Brands Hatch in his immaculate RS 2.7

They were followed past the chequered flag by a similar car crewed by Herbert Schuller with Bernhard Blank and Gunther Stekkonig. A third car entered retired with injection pump problems.

1968 had been another successful year for the 911 and it was reflected in the award of the FIA International Constructor's Trophy for G.T. cars and victory in the European Touring car challenge which they won by just 1/2 a point!

For the 1969 season the 911 started its international races with a group 3 victory in the Nurburgring 1000 kilometre race for Neuhaus/Karl Frohlich. Five 911Ts and one 911S finished and there were only three minutes between the first three cars in the 2-litre GT class by the end of the race.

In a car entered by Gaban, and driven by him and Deprez, the pair were 10th overall and won the G.T. class again at Le Mans. This time their average was 106.68 mph and 2nd in class were Chasseuil and Claude Ballot-Lena in a 911T. Seven 911s entered and four finished. Once again a G.T. class win resulted from an entry in the Targa Florio, this one driven by one Evardino Ostini.

In Belgium at the Spa 1,000 kilometres race, Gerard Larrousse and Rudi Lins ran out the G.T. winners and were 13th

R to RSR

Action! A refuelling stop for 9115609117 at the Nurburgring 1,000 kms 1975. In the background is John Fitzpatrick. Erwin Kremer supervises at the right

overall whilst at the Spa 24 hours, Claude Ballot-Lena and Chasseuil won outright.

In the European touring car challenge the 911s were this year beaten overall

Bernard Beguin and Claude Haldi shared this RSR at Spa in May 1975 to win the G.T. class and finish 4th overall

A great British effort. Nick Faure and John Cooper shared Jean Blaton's RSR 3.0 to sixth place at Le Mans 1975, chassis no. 9114609072. The RSR behind was the Asa Cachia entry driven by Borras, Noisson and Cachia. It finished 7th, chassis no. 9114609059

by the BMW 2002 turbos. There was no works entered resistance as the factory was concentrating its efforts on campaigning the big 917s.

By 1970, G.T. racing was on the wane as touring car events became more popular. It could be said that the 911's almost total domination of this class had led to its own decline but the year was still good for the car. No 2.2 litre car was homologated in group 2 but, as recounted elsewhere, the 911S was homologated in group 4.

Once again, the Nurburgring 1,000 kilometres saw the start of the season for the car and Frohlich/Toivenen took a 2.3 litre 911S to a 1st in G.T. and 14th overall, whilst 4 seconds adrift came Erwin Kremer/Huber in a similar car.

Monza – and the G.T. class winners this time were Scheretti/Zerbini (20th overall). Back to Spa for the 1,000 kilometres and Claude Haldi/Cheneviere won their class whilst being placed 16th at the finish.

For Porsche 911s, Le Mans this year was different. The factory placed its efforts behind the 914/6 in order to boost the car's image and they succeeded. One of them, crewed by Guy Chasseuil and Claude Ballot-Lena was 6th overall and won the G.T. class, this being normally a 911 prerogative. Koob and Kremer came second in the class in a 911 but they were the only ones to be placed. Six other 911Ss finished but all were excluded from the results as they didn't cover the minimum distance to qualify. Four other cars retired with various problems including the class winner of the previous two years, Gaban.

1971 dawned for the 911 with the knowledge that the factory would be supporting the 914/6, but the 911 was to show its superiority in the hands of private entrants. Using the 2.4 litre 911S, Bernard Cheneviere came fourth overall in that year's Targa Florio whilst Kremer/Huber came 12th overall and won their class in the Monza 1,000 kilometres beating Ettmuller/Sealer in a 914/6 in the process.

The Nurburgring 1,000 kilometres G.T. class was won – again – by a 911,

Right: **Bob Wollek awaits his turn to practise at Hockenheim in 1975. Note the rabbit in the passenger seat – do the regulations cover this?**

this time driven by Erwin Kremer/Neuhaus with Haldi/Keller being 12th and 13th overall. At the spa event over the same distance, Kremer and Huber triumphed again in the G.T. class whilst Schickentanz/Kerzen did the same in the Austrian 1,000 kilometres.

For Le Mans, 1971, no less than seventeen 911Ss were entered and one, entered by A.S.A. Cachia-Bondy, was 6th overall and won the G.T. class (up to 2500 cc). Driven by Tourol and "Anselme", it averaged 106.44 mph. It was followed home by six more 911Ss in 8th to 13th positions!

1972 saw the introduction of the

Clemens Schickentanz

Bob Wollek

John Fitzpatrick

73

The two main protagonists in the European G.T. Championship, George Loos (left) and Erwin Kremer

European G.T. Championship for which 911s would battle hard in the coming years and a 2.5 litre car driven by John Fitzpatrick (entrant: Kremer Racing.) dominated the series in its first year. In the first race of the series, held at the Nurburgring in conditions of pouring rain, "Fitz" as he was nicknamed, came 9th overall and beat Stekkonig and Schmid. The interesting part of this for the spectators was that when "Fitz" drove, he pulled away from the opposition but when his boss, Erwin Kremer took over, he lost the lead in his class to the "other" 911S! Fitzpatrick/Kremer finally ran out the winners of this 14 lap race. At the same venue later in the season, Fitzpatrick set a new lap record and won the race for Grand Touring cars.

In August at Hockenheim, John won the two-heat race overall and beat a field comprising Ferrari Daytonas, De Tomaso Panteras and Chevrolet Corvettes. The final race of the series was at Estoril in Portugal and "Fitz" and the Kremer Porsche won again whilst Jurgen Neuhaus in another 2.5 litre 911S came second. John Fitzpatrick's performances also resulted in him receiving the treasured Porsche cup.

The Targa Florio once again brought glory to the 911S, a 2.5 litre car placing

1974 and Helmuth Kelleners drives one of the Samson sponsored RSR 3.0 prepared by the Kremer brothers in the European G.T. championship

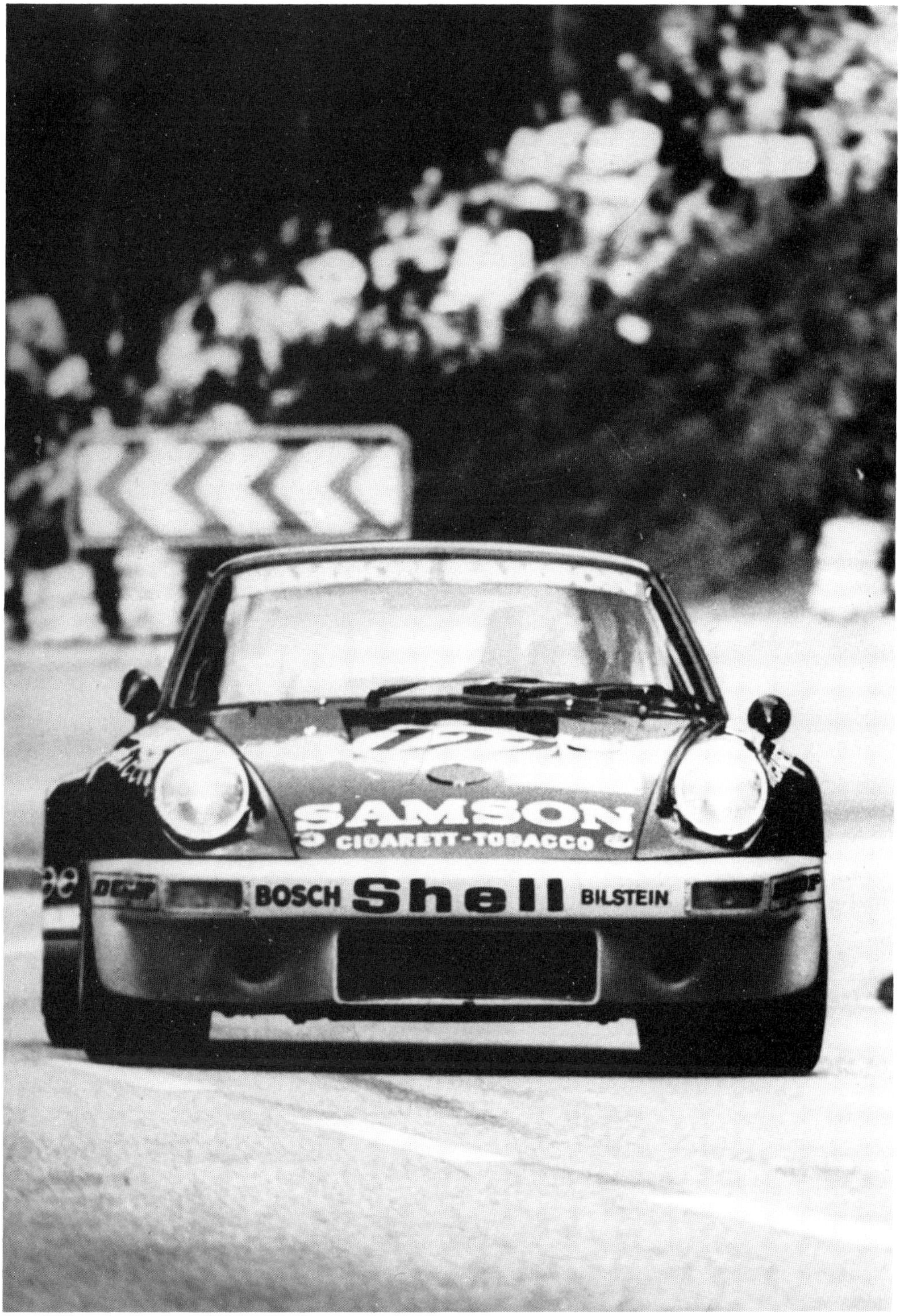
SAMSON
CIGARETT-TOBACCO
BOSCH
Shell
BILSTEIN

4th overall and winning the G.T. class. This particular entry being driven by Pica and Gottifredi.

Dr. Furhmann took over the chairmanship of the Porsche executive committee in March 1972 and from this moment the emphasis of factory supported racing swung around to the 911. From May that year work started on developing the 911 for racing further and faster than ever before.

On June 25th that year at the Osterreichring 1,000 kilometres, Gunther Stekkonig and Bjorn Waldegaard drove the first 911 with an engine capacity of 2.7 litres. As well as the bigger engine, the car also featured wider wheels and a Teldix form of A.B.S. brakes. From this car (and all the competition 911s that preceded it), the RS 2.7 Carrera was born.

In December of that year, at the Paul Ricard Circuit in France, Herbert Muller and Gijs van Lennep, together with Mark Donohue and Helmut Flegl tested the new 2.8 litre RSR. Norbert Singer was the development engineer. The main development to come out of these trials was to reposition the front stub axle higher on its strut in order to still allow the front suspension its full travel. In full group 4 trim, the development car lapped Paul Ricard in 2 minutes 10

Inset: **Jurgen Barth and John Fitzpatrick drove this RSR 3.0 into 1st place, G.T. class, at Spa in 1974**

Right: **The two Samson sponsored, Kremer prepared RSR 3.0s at Spa in 1974. The cars, driven by Schickentanz/Kauhsen and Keller/Hans Heyer finished 5th and 6th overall**

77

seconds which compared with 2 minutes 11.5 for the BMW 3.0 CSL and the Ford Capri RS, both of which were more powerful cars than the RSR.

The European G.T. Championship was held over nine races this season, starting at the Nurburgring. A two-heat race, held over two days, it was notable for Claude Ballot-Lena's victory in the first heat after John Fitzpatrick over-revved his engine and was forced out on the first lap. Despite a miraculous rebuild in the paddock overnight and John's victory in the second heat, overall victory went to Claude as he was 2nd in the last heat. Next race of the series was at the old circuit of Mon-

Austrian 1,000 kms 1974 and an RSR leads a very modified 1973 RSR 2.8 driven by Rebaque/Rojas/Van Beuren

Right: **The George Loos entered car of Fitzpatrick and Barth heads for victory in the G.T. class at the Nurburgring 750 kms in 1974**

tlhery in France and again Ballot-Lena won. However, Clemens Schickentanz was second in the last heat whilst "Fitz" again dropped out with engine problems. The 3rd twin-heat race was at Imola in Italy and here the De Tomaso Pantera driven by Mike Parkes was 1st with Schickentanz 2nd in both heats. Ballot-Lena was 3rd in both heats.

On to Nivelles, and Schickentanz won both heats with Ballot-Lena 2nd in one heat and 3rd in another (2nd was Bengt Ekberg) whilst four Panteras dropped out with burned pistons. At Estoril the first 3-litre engines appeared in the Kremer prepared cars with Paul Keller winning the 1st heat and Schickentanz

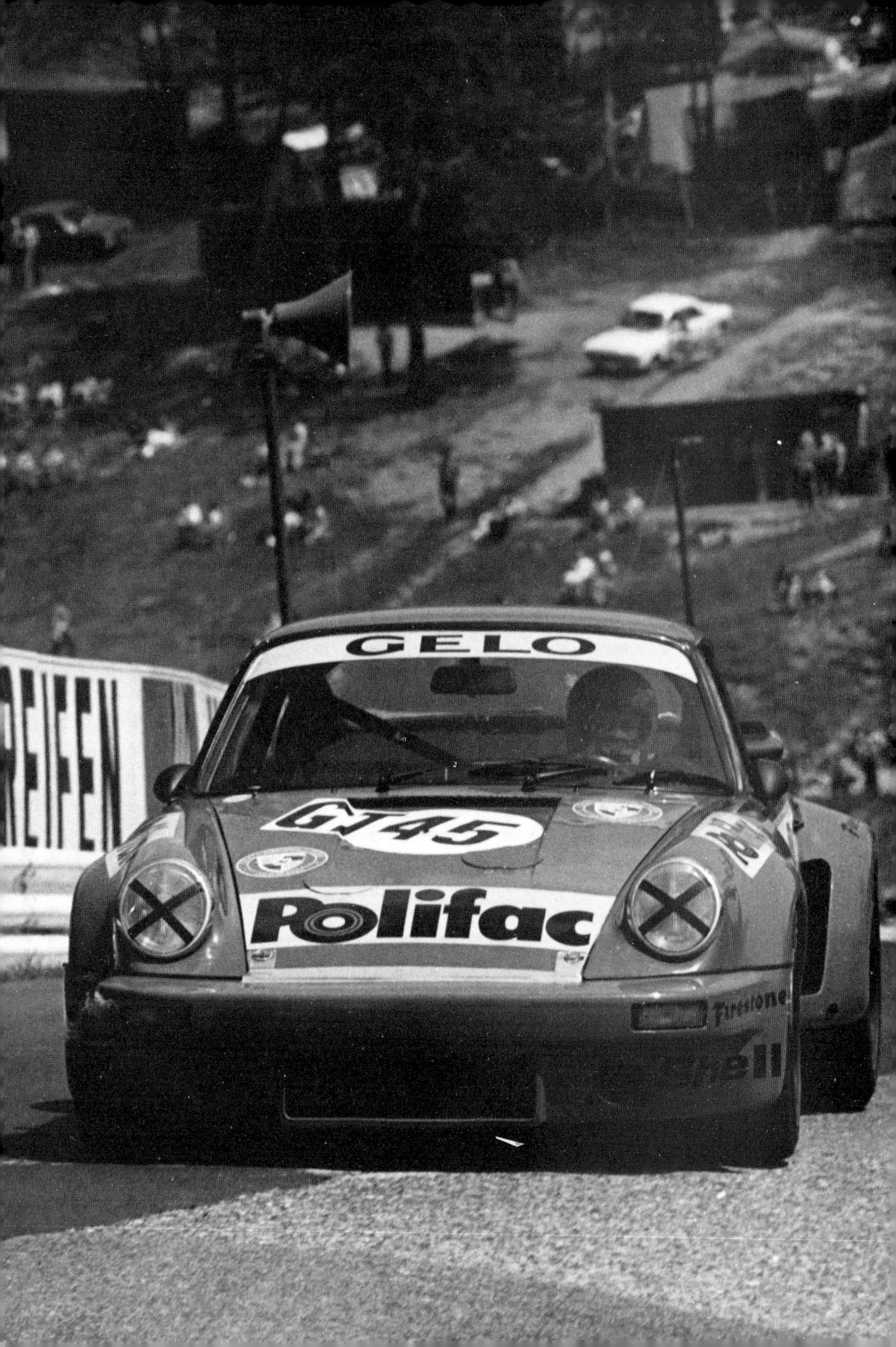
GELO
GT45
Polifac
Firestone

'At this point I was frightened!' Jay Rulon-Miller conducts his newly completed RSR 3.0 around Hockenheim in 1974

2nd. He then went on to win the 2nd heat but the overall win went to Keller. Haldi was 3rd in both heats.

In England at Thruxton it was rain all the way as Ballot-Lena and Claude Haldi finished 1st and 2nd with Schickentanz 3rd and Keller (after a spin) 4th. Once again the Panteras intervened at Hockenheim. In both heats Clay Reggazoni drove the old Mike Parkes Imola victor to repeat his performance. In trying to compete, Keller and Steckkonig damaged their engines and let Schickentanz into second place overall. Haldi was 3rd with Ballot-Lena 4th.

Below: Nurburgring 1,000 kms 1973 – the Kremer entered RSR 2.8

Freewheeling! Another photograph of 'Fitz'. In this one he is driving an RSR 2.8 in Kremer colours.

The Monza 6-Hours was next at the famous old circuit and Keller shared with Schickentanz to win. Kremer/Neuhaus were second and Ballot-Lena who was leading at this point was 5th.

Now, if the regulations had been interpreted correctly, Ballot-Lena would have had to drop the Monza result and Schickentanz would have been the series leader, but this did not happen. In the Tour de France event which followed, Schickentanz did not enter and his rival retired after leading most of the event, leaving Manucci's Lancia Stratos to win ahead of a Carrera driven by Jochen Mass/Jacques Almeras. The final race of the series was to be at MontJuich in Spain but it was cancelled! This left the FIA awarding the Championship to *both* Ballot-Lena and Schickentanz but both he and his entrant,

81

Erwin Kremer protested and after the FIA had declared there had been a "printing error' in the regulations, Schickentanz was declared the winner!

In the World championship for makes, Porsche entered two RSR's in group 5 (to avoid clashing with their customers who were mainly running in group 4) and these cars were steadily developed during the 1973 season.

Development of them actually started at the Daytona 24 hour race in February where Peter Gregg and Hurley Haywood won the event outright after the favoured prototypes had dropped out. One other RSR that retired (with a blown piston) was that of Mark Donohue and George Follmer and both of these cars were fitted with coil springs over the dampers and this now relegated the torsion bars to a supplementary role. After the race, the winning car was returned to the factory for inspection to gain test data.

Back to Europe. The two RSRs campaigned here appeared in differing trim at almost every race in Porsche's steady development and, in Martini Racing colours first competed at the Dijon 1,000 kilometre race where Herbert Muller and Gijs van Lennep finished ninth overall with Fitzpatrick/Keller 10th and Bernard Cheneviere and Peter Zbinden being 11th in 2.8 RSRs. The biggest difference with the Martini entered car was that it now contained a full 3-litre engine of 2993 cc. Of the original 2.8 litre engine, only the crankshaft and valve gear covers remained. The bore was taken out to 95 mm and this meant a new crankcase casting with the cylinder retaining studs pushed further out to accommodate the bores. This also meant new heads which had the angle between the valves decreased by $2^{1}/_{4}$ degrees to give a flatter face to the combustion chamber. Valve lift was increased to 12.2 mm for the inlets and 11.5 mm for the exhaust. Power was first estimated at 315 bhp but the substitution of slides for butterfly throttles in the intake system allowed a further 15 bhp increase in power. Over the season, the foremost of the other racing team obtained these engines.

At Spa for the 1,000 kilometre race, Muller/Van Lennep took 5th place in a car that was visually different from other RSRs. The rear ducktail aerofoil on the engine lid now continued in a line, when looking at the car from the side, into the rear wings. This, of course, gave added downforce at the rear. The air-dam at the front became deeper. George Follmer and Reinhold Joest took the other car to victory in group 4. In this race, Fitzpatrick pitted on the 1st lap but then co-drove Schickentanz's RSR to attempt to beat Follmer. It was to no avail as the engine gave up later.

Fourth place was the encouraging result at the Nurburgring 1,000 kilometeres for Muller and Van Lennep whilst the Kremer entered RSR of Paul Keller and Jurgen Nehaus won the G.T. class. Some more dramatic differences were visible at the Nurburgring. Wings were widened further to accommodate 10.5" rims at the front and 15" width at the rear whilst centre locking was used for wheel attachment on titanium hubs. Variable rate titanium coil springs were now in use around the dampers with screw-threaded abutments making changes in the rate simpler to adjust.

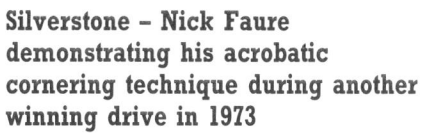

Silverstone – Nick Faure demonstrating his acrobatic cornering technique during another winning drive in 1973

Needle bearings now replaced plastic bushes in the torsion bars. All these fittings were, of course, homologated into group 4 for the use of RSR customer cars. On the Martini entered prototypes, glass reinforced plastic was used for doors and the front cover together with perspex for side and rear windows. All this brought the weight down to 1875 pounds, a full 200 less than the customer cars. At Le Mans 1973 eleven RS and RSRs entered with the group 5 car of Muller and Van Lennep finishing an outstanding 4th behind two Matras and a Ferrari 312 prototype. At the practise weekend in April, this car was timed at 179 mph down the Mulsanne straight. Of the other ten cars, Keller, Schickentanz and Kremer were the "best of the rest" in 8th place coming 2nd in the G.T. class and only being beaten by a Ferrari Daytona. Other finishers placed 10th,

Whee! Nick Faure demonstrates superb car control as he crosses the finishing line to win at Silverstone in 1973

14th, 16th and 17th whilst six retired including the other Martini car, driven by Jost/Haldi. It fell out in the 6th hour owing to a mistake in refuelling!

Monza was a disappointment for the Martini entered cars, with both of them

83

entered in the group 5 prototype class at the 1,000 kilometre race. They retired with burned pistons.

Three weeks before the 1973 Targa Florio, held this year on May 13th, a Carrera "practice car" was hurtling around the circuit with Muller/van Lennep and Kinnunen/Claude Haldi. 14 days later, another practice car and the two group 5 RSRs arrived with the team which included Steckkonig and Baron Pucci. Two 3-litre RSRs and the practice car, now with a 2.8 litre engine was the final entry. By the 4th lap, Muller and van Lennep were in a lead that they kept to win the final Targa Florio for Porsche for the 11th time. Leo Kinnunen and Claude Haldi were 3rd with Steckkonig and Pucci 6th.

One final event in Europe for the Martini entered Porsches was the Osterreichring race on June 24th and here new front air dams were fitted which really preceded the '74 shape being a complete wrap around from wheel to wheel with the oil cooler slot in the middle as normal and holes on either side to cool the brakes. One car had an experimental tail which featured longer fins on top of a flat aerofoil with the rear edge curved upwards. The flat surface of this aerofoil also held the grille for the engine cooling air intake, this being moved back from the engine cover. A bi-plane type of arrangement with side fins supporting two aerofoils was added later in testing.

This is the last we shall see of these two prototypes. With Porsche experimenting even further with more technology they reappeared in the 1974 season with turbo chargers and the company went off on another road

John Fitzpatrick conducts one of the two 2.5 litre 911Ss in a race for the European G.T. Championship in 1972

which would result in the 930 family and, as far as the 911 story goes, that ultimate in silhouette racers, the 935.

1974 saw whole races in the European G.T. championship made up of the latest "customer" car, the 3-litre RSR with its new "G" type bumper shape.

John Fitzpatrick dominated the series, winning the Porsche cup as well. Surprisingly, he drove both for the Gelo

Brands Hatch and Toine Hezemans follows Roy Pierpoint's Ford Falcon with John Fitzpatrick's Escort following in a race in 1968

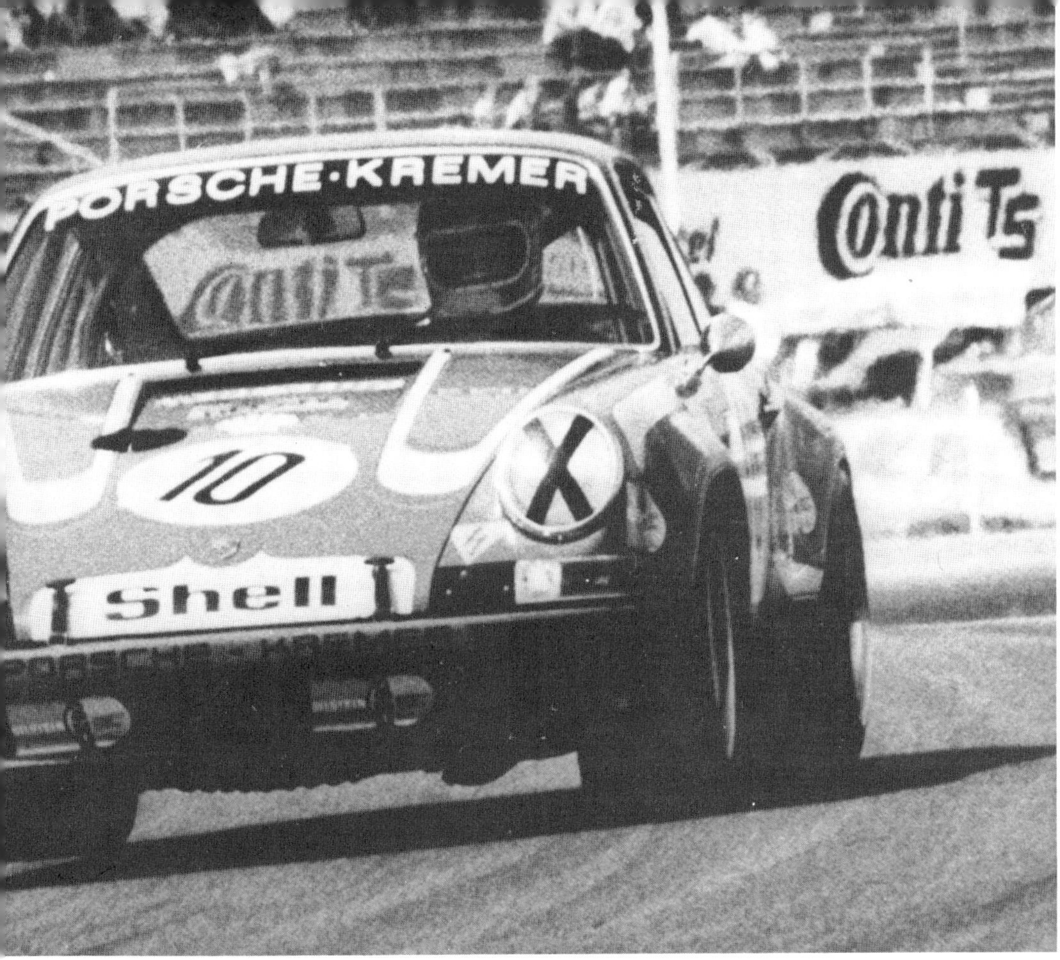
PORSCHE·KREMER
Conti TS
10
X
Shell

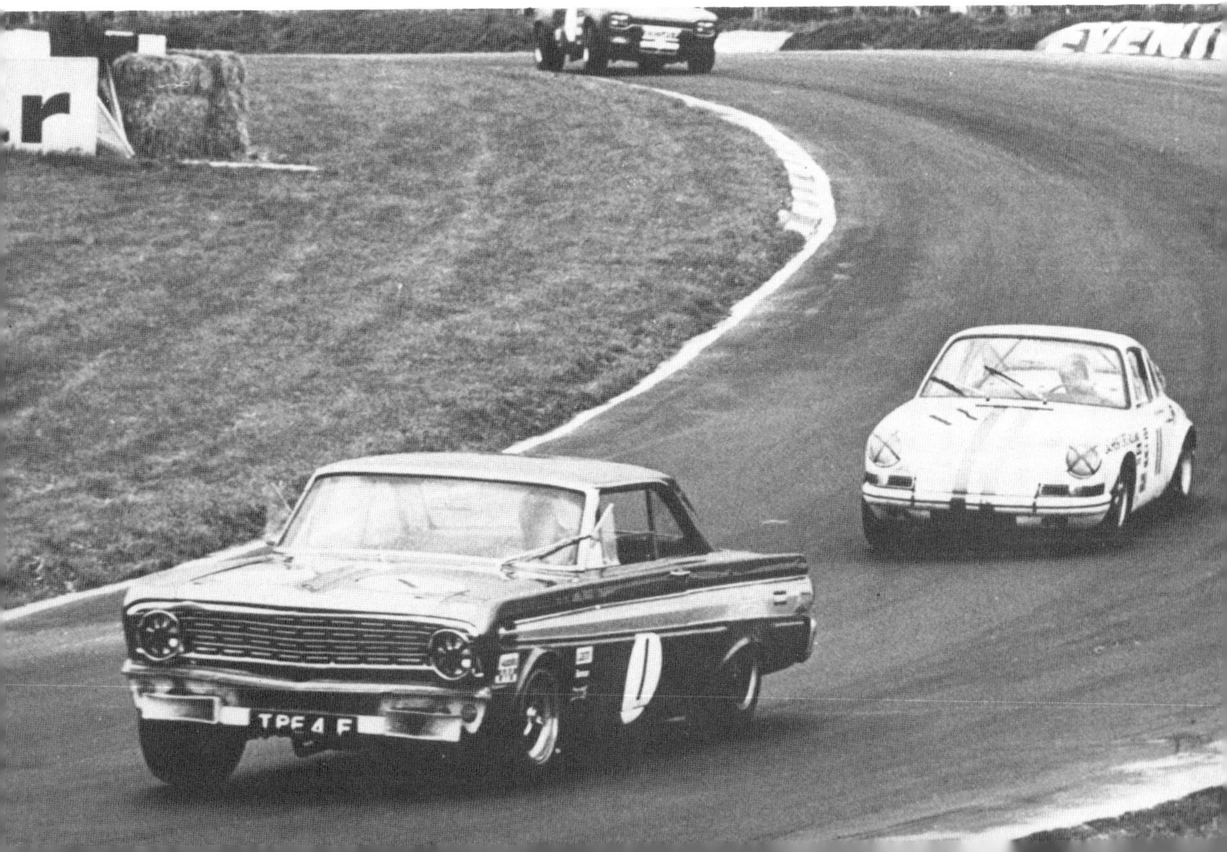
TPE 4 F

R to RSR PORSCHE

87

PORSCHE

Previous pages:

Double page: **Its the 1969 Targa Florio and a training car is practising the course**

Left side inset: **Brands Hatch and Nick Faure heads Charles Lucas who is driving Paddy McNally's 911S/T in a 1968 race**

Right side top inset: **Brands Hatch and Nick Faure leads the pack which includes Gabrielle Konig in Sprite No 125, Nick is driving the AFN demonstrator 911S with a 906 engine**

Right side bottom inset: **Gunther Knopf corners his 911S in the ADAC Bergpreis in 1967**

Below: **Hockenheim 1969 and a swarm of 911s start the 'Preis au Nutimen'**

and Kremer teams and still finished up winning! He took outright victories at Monza, Spa, Nurburgring and Kyalami. Stommelen/Schenken won the G.T. class at the Paul Ricard circuit and they then shared their car with Fitzpatrick to win at Kyalami.

The FIA cup for G.T. cars was won again for Porsche with Barth/Fitzpatrick 4th overall at Spa. RSRs also won the European Hillclimb championship and national championships in Switzerland, Sweden, Holland and France.

For 1975 the driver line-up in the championship was for Gelo: John Fitzpatrick, Tim Schenken and Toine Hezemans whilst Kremer fielded Hans Heyer and Helmuth Kelleners. The Tebernum team had Clemens Schickentanz and Hartwig Bertrams. John Fitzpatrick also raced BMWs in touring car races and this prevented him from defending his title adequately.

Imola was the first venue and, as told in John's own account, he, (Fitzpatrick) was disqualified after winning the event. Schickentanz, who had been 2nd also went the same way, leaving Claude Ballot-Lena in 1st place and Bertrams second. At the next race at the Osterreichring, RSRs filled the first twelve places! Schickentanz was 1st with Dieter Quester second and Ballot-Lena 3rd again.

Gelo wiped the floor with the opposition at the Norisring, the next race. Watched by 100,000 spectators, the team came 1st, 2nd and 3rd in the driver order of Fitzpatrick, Hezemans and Schenken. Fourth was Claude Haldi who went on to win the Hockenheim event after Schenken and Hezemans were slowed by running on rain tyres after the rain stopped and the track dried.

Another turn around at Misano in Italy saw Schenken beating Fitzpatrick by just one second with Bertrams in 3rd place whilst at the Monza 6 hour race, Bertrams, Schickentanz and Bengt Ekberg shared the winning Tebernum Porsche after the RSR driven by Fitzpatrick, Hezemans and Manfred Schurti destroyed its engine after being in the lead in the 5th hour. Merzario and Jean-Louis Chateau were 2nd. Only seven cars contested the final race at Jarama in Spain and once again the Gelo RSRs were triumphant with Schenken, Hezemans and Fitzpatrick finishing 1-2-3. The final winner of the series was Hartwig Bertrams on overall points gained.

Jean-Claude Bering won the European Hill climb championship in group 3 with an RS whilst Claude

Ballon-Lena took the French Group 4 G.T. Championship.

1976 saw the introduction of turbo power for both the Porsche 934, the group 4 G.T. car and the 935 which would go on to win Le Mans and dominate the world championships it entered. The RSRs were still entered and did well but by now they were being relegated to club races and hillclimbs where they continue to give a good account of themselves to this day.

Left: **Osterreichring 1971**

Le Mans 1971. The 911S driven by Verrier and Foucault at the chicane. This car finished 11th overall plus 8th in the index of performance

Above: **Le Mans 1971. No 35 is 911S** driven by Greub/Grant. It retired in the 20th hour. No 65 is 911S driven by De Channel/Parot, it retired in the 13th hour

R to RSR PORSCHE

Le Mans 1971 and No 40 is 911S driven by Egretaud and Jacquemin. It retired in the 8th hour – so did both the 914s following

Chapter 7
Racing in America

From the beginning of the 911, Porsche had decided that, like all its models, the car should be raced both to show its worth and to help its development. Nowhere was this to be more clearly seen than in America where the factory realized the tremendous sales potential of this market where it has always sold well.

1966 saw the 911 win the SCCA Class D production trophy, with Jerry Titus in a Vasek Polak prepared car. He was to figure large in the future of Porsche, being one of the most consistent entrants.

Daytona, fittingly enough, was the venue that saw 911s score in the international scene first of all. In 1966 they took class wins there and at Sebring and in 1968, two of them, both 911s, and driven by Ryan/Bencher and Drolsom/Williamson were 9th and 10th respectively in that year's 24 hour event whilst Porsche dealer Alan Johnson took a slightly modified "S" to take 9th overall and the G.T. class at Sebring in the 12 hour race that April.

A name that was going to be synonymous with Porsche 911 racing in the U.S. was Peter Gregg and partnered by Sten Axelsson, his first international success with the car was 9th overall and the G.T. class win in the Daytona 24 hours of 1968. Eighth overall and the G.T. class win at Watkins Glen in February followed. His partner in the six-hour event was Bob Everett.

Sebring came around again in 1969 and Alan Johnson with co-driver Gordon Kirby won the 2-litre G.T. class and were 7th overall. 911s also took the 2-litre class in the SCCA Trans-Am championship. For the next two years, the American 911s virtually mirrored the careers of their European counterparts, frequently winning the G.T. class in their capacity class in most major international events.

Things really began to hot up in 1972. As in Europe, Porsche introduced the 2.5 litre engined car to private racing teams and the two foremost teams to contest the IMSA Camel G.T. challenge were those of Toad Hall Racing, driven by Bob Beasley and Mike Keyser, and the Brumos entered cars of Hurley

Haywood and Peter Gregg.

The series was open to vehicles in the FIA's touring and Grand Touring classes. Other competing cars included Alfa-Romeos, BMWs, Datsuns, Camaros and Corvettes. Hurley Haywood won overall at Virginia International Raceway and Watkins Glen whilst he came 1st in class at Talladega. This gave him the overall G.T. Championship. Second place went to Bob Beasley. He was 1st overall at Mid-Ohio, and won his class at Donnybrooke and Daytona – twice. The contest was in doubt right to the end with Haywood leading right up to the tenth and final race at Daytona.

Beasley and Haywood had both entered two cars for their teams as they could score more points by sharing cars. Mike Keyser drove the one car whilst Tony Adamowicz had the other. Haywood was teamed with Peter Gregg in one car and Andrew Carduner in the other. Beasley won his class, coming 5th overall whilst Peter Gregg and Hurley Haywood came 6th overall and second in class. It was just enough to give Haywood a $1^1/2$ points lead over Beasley and gave him the Driver's

Watkins Glen 6 hours 1974. J. Cook/L. Heimrath lead a Ferrari Daytona to finish 4th overall and 2nd in G.T. class

95

Championship and $5,000 prize money. Porsche won the up-to-2.5-litre G.T. class at every race and at the Virginia International Race they took the first five places overall and at Lime Rock the Porsches finished 1st, 2nd, 4th and 5th overall.

But it was 1973 that saw the Porsche 911 really burst forth into the limelight. Using the new RSR and running in the prototype (group 5) class, as the car would not be homologated in group 4 until March 1st. Peter Gregg and Hurley Haywood brought their Brumos entered car into the winners circle at the Daytona 24 hour race held on February 3rd/4th.

They were only really challenged by one other 911. That was the Roger Penske entered car for Mark Donohue

February 1975 and the Brumos Porsche RSR of Peter Gregg and Hurley Haywood heads for outright victory in the Daytona 24 hour race

and George Follmer. All the Prototypes, (Ferraris, Alfas and Matras) had retired by 12.10 a.m. and Donohue/Follmer's RSR expired with a burst piston at 5.15 a.m. leaving the delighted Gregg and Haywood to cruise home to victory. At the finish, the car was so far in the lead that the Classic Car Wax Co. offered to clean and wash the car at the last pit stop, but Gregg didn't risk it!

At the end of the 1973 season, the World Championship for makes returned to the U.S.A. for the final race of the series at Watkins Glen. Once again the cars were entered by Roger Penske racing and Brumos Racing. Both cars sported the long tail spoiler as worn at the Osterreichring that year. Donohue/Follmer were sixth overall followed by Gregg/Haywood in 7th place overall. Next day, to end the season, Gregg entered the Carrera in the Can-Am race at the same venue and finished 9th.

At the end of 1973 and the beginning of 1974, Porsche had one of the best

RSR 3.0 chassis no. 9114609075 ex-Franey/Phillips. In May 1977 with Franet at the wheel it took the group's lap record at Silverstone at 106.06 mph

Engine bay of 9114609075

Left: The central-locking 917 type wheels used on RSR 3.0 cars

Below: Hartwig Bertram's RSR 9115609121, now in the USA showing its fuel cell with 'Relumit' fuel filler and vent

Opposite top: Manfred Kremer proudly shows-off the beautifully restored 9115609117

Opposite bottom: The front compartment of RSR 3.0 9115609117 showing the long-range fuel tank and strengthening strut between the suspension towers

Inset: The brake air-exit slots on the front wings of a 1975 RSR

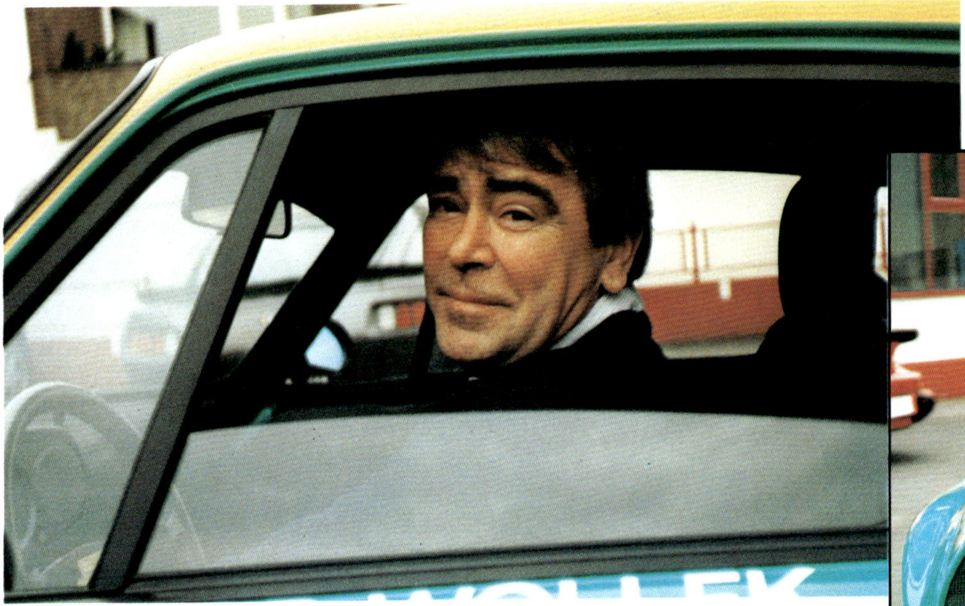

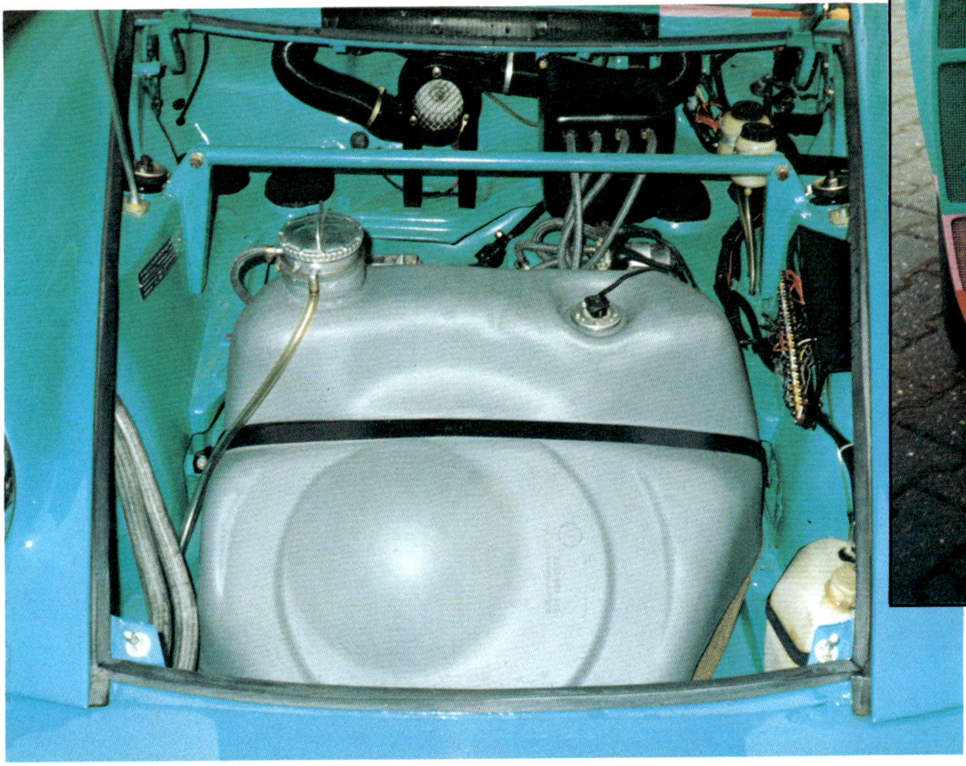

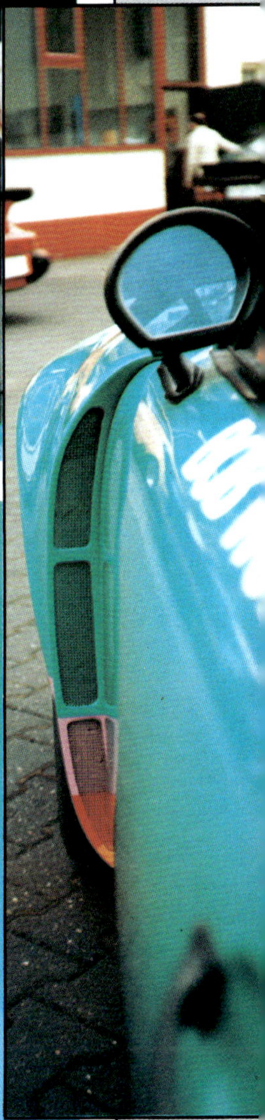

R to RSR PORSCHE

Fuel tank, and piping to front mounted oil cooler in 9115609117
Glorious! The power-house of a 1975 RSR 3.0 with slide injection and twin ignition

The two Kremer-prepared 2.5 911S's for 1972. The cars were driven by John Fitzpatrick and Erwin Kremer.

R to RSR PORSCHE

Eleven of the IROC RS/RSR 3.0 cars at Riverside behind the 914 pace car. Donohue in the white car leads with Revson on his right. Denny Hulme is behind in No. 6 whilst Pearson is in No. 5

R to RSR PORSCHE

The author's 'racer' – part 3.0 RS, part RSR plus a 935 front!

The RSR engine of the author's 'racer' 911. Chassis no. 91136090357, engine capacity is now 3.2 litres and reputed to develop 350 bhp!

beginnings to a sales year in the USA that they could possibly have had. Roger Penske, in conjunction with Mike Phelps and Les Richter, The Riverside Raceway promoter, put on a series of races, three at Riverside and a finale at Daytona called the "International Race of Champions" or IROC for short. The series was televised by the ABC network.

The promoting trio bought 15 of the new 1974 model RSs with RSR engines. Their chassis numbers were: 016, 025, 035, 037, 040, 042, 050, 059, 075, 085, 090, 100, 111, 116 and 124. All prefixed with 9114609. They were to be delivered to Riverside in time for first practise for the first event. Twelve of them were sent by sea whilst the remaining three practise cars were airfreighted later. To drive these cars, Penske enrolled a "Who's Who" of European and American driving talent. They were: Mark Donohue, George Follmer, Peter Revson, Denny Hulme, Emerson Fittipaldi, Roger McCluskey, Richard Petty, David Pearson, A.J. Foyt, and Gordon Johncock. Al Unser and Mario Andretti could not join in, owing to their Firestone contracts.

The cars were built and adjusted to be as close as possible to one another to keep the racing close and to this end, engines gave 316 bhp with 9" front and 11" rear wheel widths. The cars were painted brilliantly different from one another, in order that the spectators could tell who was who, and Porsche logos adorned the sides and bumpers of the cars. Goodyear supplied the low profile racing tyres. The cars were actually shipped with RS 2.7 type "ducktail" spoilers but these were changed in time for the first race to the "teatray" type flat spoiler. The Riverside races were of 75 miles each and it took the Daytona Final to decide the winner. To nobody's real surprise, it was Mark Donohue. He announced his (premature) retirement after the final race and put $41,000 for 93.9 miles of racing into his bank account. Even A.J. Foyt, who blew his engine on the second lap after attempting to change down from 5th gear and collecting second instead, picked up $9,900! Donohue's winning average at Daytona, which included an infield section to slow the cars, was 114.97 mph.

In the IMSA Camel G.T. Trophy, Peter Gregg drove a 3-litre RSR complete with centrifugal air extractors on the wheels to win. It was an outstanding year for him. Tough opposition was present with works entered BMWs and some very fast Corvettes but although one of these, driven by John Greenwood, won the Trans-Am series, this series had declined in popularity due to attention being paid to the Camel sponsored G.T. series. This also supplied Gregg with the Porsche plus Audi GT cup USA as well as a prize fund of $29,400.

Gregg's prowess and ability in the RSR gave him victory yet again and his third consecutive Camel G.T. championship in an RSR. His erstwhile partner, Hurley Haywood now drove his own RSR to challenge "the boss" but he failed by 11.5 points overall.

The season opened with the Daytona 24 hours and Haywood partnered Gregg in the former's well known number 59 for the race. They led home a Porsche 1st to 6th place victory parade with the faster BMWs and Corvettes dropping out with mechanical failures. The highlight of Haywood's race was after Gregg had lost time through a collision with a back marker which damaged his door and front wing. With fog descending through the night and the rest of the field slowing down, Haywood maintained his pace to put the Brumos RSR 15 laps ahead at the finish.

Six weeks later came the 12-hours of Sebring and the faster BMWs stayed together to win. Brian Redman and Allan Moffat were the drivers, whilst Gregg and Haywood were forced to retire after Gregg once again hit a backmarker. This time the damage included a twisted floorpan which, as far as this race was concerned, was terminal.

Two 100 mile heats were run at Road Atlanta, each treated as individual races. Porsche RSRs won both heats with no BMW or Corvette opposition entering. Gregg won the first while Al Holbert, a driver who had had bad luck in the first two races, and had led Daytona until his engine failed, won a deserved second heat.

Laguna Seca saw a repeat of the two race system and Gregg won the first heat again, beating Hans Stuck in the factory BMW CSL to the flag whilst the BMW turned the tables in the second race to win, putting Gregg into 4th place after an unexpected pit stop.

In Southern California, at Riverside Raceway, the next race was over six hours and on this fast course, the BMWs of Hans Stuck/Dieter Quester and Brian Redman/Sam Posey finished 1st and 2nd ahead of Gregg in 3rd place.

The RSRs turned the tables at Lime Rock Park in two more 100 mile heats when Gregg led from start to finish in the first event from his pole position. Gregg and Holbert held off the two works BMWs for the second heat until Gregg spun on the very last lap letting Holbert win but recovering to finish 2nd ahead of the BMWs.

Al Holbert won both heats of the next race at the Mid-Ohio track. He was, however helped in the second heat when both Stuck and Gregg retired with wheel bearing problems. Haywood was 3rd.

A crowd of 50,000 turned out when the series came to Canada for the first time. The venue was Mosport Park and the finish of the two 50 mile heats dictated the starting order for the main race of 98 miles. The BMW of Brian Redman beat Gregg in the first heat by $3/10$ths of a second whilst Holbert won the second. The BMW led the longest race until its engine proved unreliable and then a Camaro led and pushed Gregg off course. Haywood took advantage of this and the Camaro's handling to just pip it to the finish.

The BMWs struck back at Daytona on the fourth of July where Stuck won with Haywood second while Gregg uncharacteristically retired the RSR when his engine broke a valve. At Mid-America it was Holbert again in the first heat with Gregg second and Haywood third. In the second heat, the finishing order was the same although each of the three above took turns in the lead until Haywood retired with transmission trouble. Then Gregg had a puncture and finished a distant 2nd.

Rainy weather troubled Talladega,

An RSR 3.0 racing in an IMSA event. Note the air dam flush with the front bumper. Driver is probably Peter Gregg for the Brumos team

one of the fastest speedways in the world but incorporating an infield section for the next race. The race started in the dry and Stuck used his horsepower to pull away in the BMW with Gregg in 2nd place. Rain then stopped the race. When it started again, Stuck drew away to a 30 second lead over Gregg and Haywood and that's the way it finished when the race was stopped again at half distance owing to the rain returning.

Al Holbert won the Mid-Ohio 6-hour race after Gregg and Haywood had led and pulled away in a new long tailed RSR that had shades of the 935 turbo Porsche about its looks. Then the old Gregg bugbear of colliding with a slower car and the hour long pit stop that resulted dropped the entry to 9th at the finish although they had been as low as 16th at one point.

Daytona saw the final event of the series and the RSRs were beginning to show their age. On this fast track, horsepower told and a Chevrolet Corvette driven by John Greenwood won. The BMWs of Redman and Posey were 2nd and 3rd with Gregg's car 4th and Haywood 5th. So Peter Gregg won a series with what was, by now, an outdated car. It just showed what could be done with those great qualities the Porsche RSR possessed. Strength and reliability.

At Daytona the second Brumos entered RSR, driven by Carl Schafer had several important changes under the skin which was itself even thinner than normal. The car had Turbo RSR rear suspension and a front mounted oil tank but Schafer only managed 11th place with it. Gregg sold this car to Jim Busby as he was driving for BMW in 1976. Busby won four 1976 races with it even though new rules forced the car to carry ballast to reach the minimum weight. Al Holbert and Mike Keyser won Sebring whilst George Dyer won at

Lime Rock. Even into 1977 the Carreras were still entering and winning in SCCA racing. Like old soldiers, RSRs never died, they just faded away where top class racing was concerned.

Hurley Haywood

I started racing with Peter Gregg in 1969 with a 2.2 litre Porsche 911S. We raced it in a world championship race up at Watkins Glen and won our class against Corvettes and the big machinery. That's what you call jumping in at the deep end!

I was at college in Florida and that's where I met up with Peter Gregg. I had a Corvette at the time and I used to race it in Autocrosses. Peter and I tied for first place in one event and had to have a run-off. He was testing some parts on his race car and I beat him and that's how we became friends. I had talked my father into supporting me in motor racing and he gave me a two-year timetable. Peter was the one who took everything in hand and so he was the one I ordered my first race car from.

The first year I was in racing we raced a 911S and then I spent one year in the military in Vietnam in 1970 and when I came back we switched over to the 914/6 and raced that car.

We alternated between a 911 and the 914 until 1972 and then in 1973 it was the first year the factory came out with the RSR which we raced and won with at Daytona.

The RS and the RSR were really greatly improved versions of the previous racing 911s. The first car I raced was a practically stock 911; it was race-prepared but had no really tricky racing parts on it. The RSR which we raced in 1973 was all tricked up for racing; there was a very big difference between these cars.

In 911s, my most satisfying victory was the first time I won at Daytona (with Peter Gregg in 1973 in the RSR 2.8); it was by biggest thrill and what with going to the Sebring 12 hours and winning that, also in the same year in an identical car, well, that was a big shot!

I was basically nobody at that point and suddenly I win two of the most prestigious races in the world; so it was a good boost for my career and I know Peter had worked for it for a long time, so I think that that was terrific.

Looking back, I realize that I didn't have enough years of experience in the business to appreciate just what we had accomplished, but now, I realize just what a difficult feat that was.

When we raced with a 911 the competition was other 911s, several good cars in very capable hands. Al Holbert had a car, George Dyer, the Toad Hall racing team with Mike Keyser; the racing was spectacular. In addition were the big-engined Corvettes and two Camaros. BMWs didn't really come up with a competitive car until 1976. I drove that car as Peter (Gregg) had switched camps and it was a really wonderful car. It certainly gave Porsche a run for its money.

We sold quite a few RSRs from the Brumos dealership. Peter took delivery and sold them as an agent for Porsche much in the fashion that Al Holbert is doing now. We really created our own opposition but were always one step ahead of them! Peter had a very good relationship with the factory and received goodies on our car that we proved in the races and then these improvements were passed on to the customers.

A 911 was always a treacherous car to drive. Certainly it was difficult with the weight over the back wheels and in the wet it was worse! It was something that all 911 drivers adapted to. When you had confidence you could throw the car around fairly well and not have it get away from you but it took some practise! However, once you gained confidence in the car you could toss it around; it was really fun to drive. I crashed a 911 at Watkins Glen after a misunderstanding with another driver going up to turn 2 on the old circuit. We came together and the car vaulted over the guard rail and landed nose-first on the other side. That was a pretty big wreck!

If I had had the foresight to keep all the race cars that I have been privileged to drive, I'd be a multi-millionaire now. You know, you never think about it when you're in that position, those cars are now worth a lot of money!

Chapter 8
Rallying

Although Porsche had already used its 911 with great success in rallies from the type's introduction, as witness Herbert Linge and Peter Falk taking a mildly modified car to 5th place in the 1965 Monte Carlo Rally. It wasn't really until the advent of the 911S that they really started to make headway in this field of motorsport.

Having stated this, however, Porsche went on to win the European G.T. Rally Championship in 1966 with Gunther Klass being the Champion. With his navigator, Wutherich, he was 1st overall in the German Rally and 1st in the G.T. class in the Alpine Rally. A broken throttle cable stopped them in the Geneva event.

1967 was the year that the 911S was homologated for international competition and the Swede, Bjorn Waldegaard led his own country's rally until the gearbox broke. Sobieslaw Zasada, who with that name could only be a Pole, won the Austrian Alpine Rally in a works 911S and then took his own 911 to South America and won the Argentine Grand Prix, a 2,000 mile Rally. But by far the best performances were undoubtedly put up by Vic Elford who, in the few rallies in which he drove owing to his racing commitments, managed to win the Geneva, Tulip and Lyons-Charbonnieres (this heading a 911 1-2-3-4.) Rallies as well as finishing 3rd in the Monte Carlo Rally with his navigator, David Stone. All this was good enough to give the factory the group 3 European G.T. rally championship for that year.

Two homologated 911Ts, now with "S" power of 180 bhp, were given to Vic Elford and David Stone and Paoli Toivenan and his navigator, Tiuhkanen for the first Rally of 1968, the Monte Carlo. With the low axle ratio giving 104 mph at the 7200 rpm limit, a 26.4 gallon fuel tank and a 75% limited slip differential fitted, they stormed on to 1st and 2nd places overall, respectively. The navigator was even equipped with a floor mounted horn push!

Paoli Toivenen then went on to win the Geneva, East German, Danube, Spanish, San Remo and the German rallies to bring the World and European

6th place overall in the 1975 Manx Rally went to this RS 2.7 lightweight driven by John Price and Mike Songs. The car has an RS 3.0 'teatray' spoiler

Rally Championship to him as the driver and Porsche as the entrant. Waldegaard, with his navigator, Lars Helmer, succeeded in winning the Swedish Rally this time.

For the 1969 season, Waldegaard succeeded in repeating this victory as well as winning the Monte Carlo Rally, this time using a long wheelbase 911T. Gerard Larrousse was second and both drivers were reported as not liking the handling of the new long wheelbase fuel injected cars as much as the previous short wheelbase models. In fact, Waldegaard had resorted to his previous year's car to win the Swedish event. Toivenen used a 1969 car to win the Acropolis Rally whilst Zasada won the Polish Rally again.

The "Tour de France" event (Rally or race we're not sure, but it included a marathon trek around France with at least six races and three Hillclimbs as well as timed road sections in six days) was revived in September and was won by Larrousse with Maurice Gelin as his co-driver in a 911R. They went on to win the Tour de Corse, this time reputedly with a four-cam racing engine fitted after one had blown up on the Lyons Charbonniere Rally. All this, however, was not enough to win the Constructor's championship for Porsche and in fact they finished 2nd that year.

The Monte Carlo Rally was, naturally, the first event of 1970 and Porsche gave two 235 bhp 2.3 litre group 4 cars to Waldegaard/Helmer and Larrousse/Gelin. On the last stage, Waldegaard actually used racing tyres to pull away from Larrousse and win. Waldegaard then used a less powerful car to win the Swedish Rally just four weeks later and, in so doing, made it a hat-trick of victories for himself and the 911. He then took the same car to win the Austrian Alpine Rally.

Claude Haldi claimed 2nd overall in

103

R to RSR

the Lyons-Charbonniere event whilst Janger won the Danube Rally, and Gass/Frey the Bodensee Rally. Porsches did not finish the Acropolis Rally due to broken engines whilst Waldegaard and Anderson lost all drive to the wheels in that year's RAC Rally. One of the service cars on this event was actually Larrousses' Tour De France car, an ST chassis no: 911030949, fitted now with a 2.5 litre engine instead of the 2.4 litre one Larrousse had used.

Left: **The original AFN demonstrator, chassis no. 9114609100 in the Manx Rally 1975. The car finished 8th overall**

Below left: **Dessie McCartney and Terry Harryman during the 1975 Manx Rally. The car has RS 3.0 bodywork but reputedly had a 2.8 engine. They finished 2nd.**

The car was driven by someone who would become much better known as a driver of works Porsches in years to come, Jurgen Barth. When Larrousse had used the car on the "Tour de France", it had been the lightest 911 ever at 789 kilogramme weight. Larrousse promising the Porsche engineers a bottle of champagne for every kilogramme under 800 and he finished up giving them 11 bottles of best French Champagne! It was left to Larrousse to finish 6th (two points) in the RAC Rally to bring the European G.T. Championship home to Porsche.

Porsche's interest in major league rallies dwindled from this point on as, beside concentrating their major efforts

Below: **The 2.7 RS Carrera abounded as a private entry in rallies. Here Graham Waldron is on his way to a class 2nd in the 1975 RAC Rally**

Right: **A smiling Roger Clark drives 'Piggy' at the finish of the Lombard RAC Rally. The car is battered but did finish! Note the windscreen hold-in clips.**

Far right: **The lightest ever 911. The Larrousse/Gelin 'Tour de France' car of 1970**

Below: **Waaldegaard on his way to victory in the 1970 Swedish Rally. The car is a works entered 911S**

into World Championship Racing with the ferociously powerful 917s and even more powerful Can-Am Turbocharged variants, they realized that 911s in G.T. racing were actually a more cost-effective method of promoting the sale of their road-going 911s. They also transferred their rally effort for this year to the 914/6 but had little success.

2nd place in the 1970 Monte Carlo Rally was this 911S driven by Larrousse/Gelin

R to RSR PORSCHE

Right inset: **Lyons-Charbonniere Rally 1970. The car is the Monte Carlo Rally winner**

Far right inset: **The start of the 1970 Monte Carlo Rally for Waaldegaard/Helmer – the eventual winners**

Main picture: **Gerard Larrousse and Maurice Gelin cornering hard in the 1969 Tour de Corse in a 911R. The car has a four-cam engine and they went on to victory**

In fact Waldegaard only finished 3rd in that year's Monte Carlo Rally whereas he thought he could have won had he been given a 911S. He was given one of these for that year's RAC Rally and together with Nystrom, his navigator, bought it home in 2nd place overall.

Porsche did enter three very modified 2.4 litre cars for Waldegaard, Zasada and Andersson in the East African Safari Rally. These cars had 180 bhp engines and final drives which limited top speed to 112 mph. Suspensions were lifted to give the cars the

The winner! Waaldegaard displays the spoils of his 1969 victory

AUTOMOBILCLUB
AvD
VON DEUTSCHLAND
START
AUTOMOBILCLUB
AvD
VON DEUTSCHLAND
DUNLO
RALLYE MONTE-CA
S-T 5706
Shell
S-K 2403

The scene is the Acropolis Rally in 1968. The car is a 911L and the drivers are Zasada and Dobrzanski

maximum amount of ground clearance and the cars carried a substantial amount of spares. Andersson retired with rear suspension breakage whilst Waldegaard went off the road and was unable to continue. It was left to Zasada to finish the event in 5th place. At one point he had been 2nd but a misfiring engine dropped him down the field.

1972 saw Waldegaard being beaten into 2nd place in the Swedish Rally in a private 911S through a wrong choice of tyres whilst Larrousse similarly finished 2nd in the Monte Carlo Rally that year. Yet another 2nd place went to Zasada in one of the Safari "Specials" on the East African Classic and he likewise came 2nd in the driver's Championship.

By 1974 the RS Carrera was being used by many privateers in rallying and an Irish contingent proved very successful. In that country two RS2.7s

Stuttgart-Lyon Rally 1967. Zasada plunges through a snowstorn on his way to 3rd place

Before the start of the 1967 Marathon de la Route. From left to right: Hans Schuller, Terry Hunter, Vic Elford, 'Pedor' and Jean-Pierre Gaban

driven and navigated by Cahal Curley/ Austin Frazer and Ronnie McCartney/ Peter Scott were 1st and 2nd on the Circuit of Ireland Rally. Cahal Curley and his navigator then went on to win the Manx Trophy Rally and the Donegal International event giving him the title

Vic Elford and co-driver at the start of the 1967 Marathon de la Route in a 911R. They went on to win the 84 hour event

of Irish Rally Champion. The Galway International Rally was won by yet another 2.7RS driver, Dessie McCartney, Ronnie's brother.

The Safari Rally still beckoned Porsche drivers and this year Waldegaard drove another 2.7RS modified and with raised suspension.

Another, similar, car was driven by Bill Fritschy and the cars were sponsored by Chipstead of Kensington. After two suspension breakages, Waldegaard finally finished 2nd, whilst Fritschy retired when an oil pipe sheared.

Now well and truly committed to circuit racing with the RSRs, Porsche took a very definite back seat as far as rallies were concerned but this did not stop hordes of private owners entering their 911s in all sorts of rallies.

One of the biggest surprises for the factory, therefore, was to learn that a 911 had won the Monte Carlo Rally for the fourth time! This event occurred as late as 1978 when, driving what is described as an "SC" but which we believe could have been a 3.0RS, Jean-Pierre Nicholas, navigated by Vincent Laverne won the prestigious event in an Almeras Freres entered car. One final fling at the Safari Rally was taken this year with RSs. Using, this time, 3-litre engines in modified SCs with no less than 11" of ground clearance, Porsche employed, once again, Bjorn Waldegaard and Lars Thorszelius with Vic Preston Jr. and Lyall in the sister car. Both cars were sponsored by Martini.

Once again it was not to be. Waldegaard broke, among other parts, a rear suspension arm and replacing this put him down into 4th place. Vic Preston

Victory in the 1967 Geneva Rally for Vic Elford/David Stone in works 911S

did better. Despite broken drive shafts and worn-out dampers, he managed a creditable 2nd place to bring down the curtain on the 911s international rallying career.

However, such is the suitability of the car to "tail-out" driving styles, 911s are still being entered in rallies and placing well up to national levels.

A works entry in the 1967 Coupe des Alpes

Early days: 1966 and a bent 911 continues in the Corsica Rally

Vic Elford and David Stone in their works entered 911S in the 1967 Corsican Rally

Chapter 9
Driving Porsche

What is it like to own and drive an RS or RSR today? The answer to the latter is tremendous and to the former, expensive! I will elaborate.

As I explained in the Foreword, my real experience of RSs is devoted to the 3-litre model, having owned one Autofarm "replica" and one "real" car.

The latter has now been joined by a racer that started life as an RS 2.7 litre car, a perfectly standard lightweight, (if there is such an animal!) and then was returned to the factory in 1978 to be brought up to "G" standard RS 3-litre guise. The reason for this was that the owner, a Herr Klaus Utz, decided that he would like to contest the German National sports car championship. This was roughly the equivalent of our "Intermarque" series and he contested thirteen events that season with the car.

The uprated RS now sported one more dramatic difference from standard 3-litre form. Its tail now held a full works RSR engine complete with "big-bore" injection, slides instead of butterfly throttles and twin plug injection complete with transistorised ignition.

At the time of writing, I have no idea how the car fared, but it was then imported into this country at the beginning of 1979 and did sundry races, including two six-hour events, one at Snetterton and one at Brands Hatch with John Harper and John Beasley driving. It finished 11th overall at Brands Hatch.

After this, the car was bought by Roland Jones, a keen hill-climb entrant and he embarked on a major weight losing exercise of the car. What's the secret of success with a racing car? Add power and gain lightness. Roland certainly succeeded with the latter. The car's front wings and doors were removed. These were replaced in thin fibreglass and the side and rear window's glass was replaced by perspex. Even the hinges and locks of the doors were drilled out for lightness! The passenger seat was removed and a proper racing bucket seat with four-point safety harness and headrest was substituted for the original driver's seat. A full fire extinguisher system was plumbed in for safety whilst a tiny two gallon fuel tank replaced the long distance tank that originally resided in the front compartment.

The engine received new barrels and pistons which raised its capacity to 3.2 litres and a reputed 350 bhp is now delivered. Having seen the car depart the start line of Prescot Hillclimb on several occasions and felt the ground shake beneath its wheels, I can well believe this! Incidentally, the car holds the record over the first 60 yards of Prescot as the fastest accelerating car entered at that famous venue.

After several successful seasons in the hands of Roland Jones and John and Sue Hunt, the car received an engine rebuild after an overrevving disaster and I acquired the car at the end of 1986. I wanted to circuit race the car in the Inter-Marque series and, to that end, I have had the long-range tank and the engine oil-cooler refitted. As lighting is required by the rules, these have also been replaced, the headlamps now residing in the airdam at the front. To drive, this car performs in a very similar manner to a road-going 911, just faster! 0-60 mph has been timed at 3 seconds so everything occurs rapidly. I look forward to the 1987 season with a mixture of excitement and fear! When the season is over, I intend to replace the original body panels which came with the car and turn the car back to a 3.0 RS.

The second car is an original RS 3.0 which I acquired in a part exchange for a replica RS 3.0 which I had bought from Autofarm. Confusing, isn't it! This was actually a very nice car indeed and with full carpeting and a sports exhaust, it was an extremely pleasant car in which to travel any journey, be it on motorways or across country.

This car possessed a twin-plug engine and big bore injection but with butterfly throttles and was said to deliver around 280 bhp which certainly seemed believable in view of its terrific performance. The car was shod with Pirelli P6 tyres of the original specification size and I can only say that it felt very undertyred, (particularly in the wet!) I hillclimbed the car several times and took it to Donington for a Porsche practise day but found to my chagrin that an "ordinary" RS 2.7 could stay with me on the straight although it was a different matter when it came to cornering. I could always outbrake the 2.7 litre car and outcorner it. Not surprising in view of the 917 brakes and wider tyres! I telephoned Josh Sadler of Autofarm about the speed (or lack of) of the car in a straight line when considering its power and his reply was simply: "I'm not surprised. Last year we had a car with 300 bhp and it was only one second a lap faster than a 2.7. It's the big wheel arches and airdam of the RS 3.0 that slow it down!"

The next Porsche to arrive in our garage was a real RS 3.0 which had been 12th overall at the 1976 Le Mans 24 hour race and won the G.T. class. I saw the car advertised in *"Motor Sport"* and went to look at it. Compared with the replica car, it was in very sad shape. After negotiation involving trading the replica, I proudly drove the car home.

As soon as I was on the way home. I realised that the car needed an awful lot of work. The engine misfired, the gearbox howled when travelling at over 80 mph and the gearchange was

The author's own RS 3.0 featured in a window 'sticker' and affixed to an RS 2.7 Carrera – somewhere in France!

incredibly sloppy. All this as well as bodywork with wheel arches well out of shape and a tendency for the car to sit down at one corner when viewing the car on the level. The one good thing was that the brakes worked!

So to a rebuild. Upon stripping, the valve springs of most of the cylinder heads were found to be broken. Also, one cylinder and piston were too scored to keep and a new matching pair were obtained from Mahle. We had to wait a considerable time for these as they are special high compression items. The rest of the engine was in good condition and was put back together with new gaskets, etc. The gearbox was stripped and the oil pump was found to be broken. A new one was substituted along with new synchromesh rings. The original limited slip differential was missing and a new one was made up by Dave Richards Autosport who had been campaigning the 911 SC RS Rothmans Rally team the year before.

The bodywork was stripped to bare metal and the wheel arches were beaten back into shape. The nose of the car was also reshaped to accept the glass fibre bumper cum airdam, which, when I bought the car, had ripples across its top surface.

After all of this, the car was repainted in Grand Prix white and had new black "Carrera" decals applied to its sides and an "Almeras Freres" (the company who entered the car at Le Mans) decal applied to the front bumper. This car has an extremely low back axle ratio giving 19 mph per 1,000 rpm with a top speed of approximately 138 mph. One hundred miles an hour seems to come up as fast as one can move one's hand on the gear lever!

To drive, this car is exhilarating. From the time that you slide into the Sparco seat that appears to enfold you and renders reversing extremely difficult, to squirming from the car at the end of the journey, life is taken up with passenger complaints of strained neck muscles when using the car's massive acceleration and braking. As the driver is solely occupied coping with and enjoying the incredible grip offered by Pirelli P7 tyres of 285/40/15 size on the rear and 225/50/15 on the front, the passenger's cries go largely unheeded! Though the grip of the tyres and the efficiency of the braking appear enormous, it must be said that I have spun the car on no less than three occasions at test days on race tracks. I put this down to a mixture of enthusiasm, stupidity and a capacity to use up all of the car's braking and roadholding limits as the RS simply encourages the driver to use them!

And so we come to the end of the saga of the racing cum roadgoing 911s. Through the ten years of 1967 to 1977 these exciting, vibrant cars gave enormous pleasure to the crowds who flocked to racing circuits and rally courses, excited and enthused their drivers and brought the Porsche factory yet more victories in its competition orientated career.

Though the 911 would develop into the 930 turbo and its 934 and 935 racing derivatives, the Carrera RS and RSRs have shown themselves to be, with the passing of time, all time classics.

John Fitzpatrick

In 1967 I first drove a 911 at the Nurburgring 6-hours. It was – tricky! I drove with Ben Pon. We were leading the race with an hour to go, but then a bolt broke in the rear suspension and we finally finished well down.

In 1972 Erwin Kremer entered me for the European G.T. Championship in a 2.5 litre car. I don't think the 911 had had much development since I had last driven one. Again the Nurburgring was the first race of the series and I remember that it poured with rain the whole weekend. I won quite a few races that year and collected the Porsche cup as well as the G.T. Championship. That was a busy year as I also took part in the World Championship of makes as well as driving Schnitzer-entered BMW 3.0 CSLs in the Touring car Championship. In fact they were probably a bit quicker than the 2.5 litre 911s of that year.

The following year, 1973, Porsche came out with the 2.7 Carrera and I drove a 2.8 RSR again entered by Kremer, but I only did three or four races for him and had a lot of bad luck in the first two. I was also driving Ford Capris that year and although I achieved one or two good results with them, they were a real handful, I much preferred the Porsche, it handled a lot better!

The real quantum leap in 911 race car performance came with the 1974 3.0 litre RSR because in that year they had a different rear wing and much wider wheels. This was a really good car and it was built by the factory itself whereas up to 1972 all the race cars had been built by outside shops like Kremer who bought the parts from Porsche. I can't remember the times but it (the 1974 RSR) was quite a few seconds a lap quicker everywhere than the 1973 car.

On the driving side, I started off the season with Kremer paying me to drive for him and he also had Paul Keller paying him to drive another RSR for him. After 3 or 4 races I had had quite a few mishaps and didn't have any points for the Championship and as I didn't have a chance of winning the Championship, Erwin Kremer told me he wasn't prepared to carry on paying me any more. So I stopped as I wasn't prepared to pay for my racing! So Keller stayed with Kremer for 1974 and he also took on Schickentanz who was quite good then.

So, at the start of 1974, George Loos asked me to drive for his Gelo team on a professional basis and I started to win straight away. We also did the G.T. Championship and the 1,000 kilometre races again. George Loos was an incredibly difficult man to drive for. When he drove, he used to resent the fact that anyone, not just me, could drive the same car faster than him. He would bring in other drivers such as Merzario and Vic Elford to get at me because I was beating him. I got fed up with him around Le Mans time and I decided not to drive for him any more even though I was leading the Championship at that stage.

Once I had won a few races in 1974, Kremer could see that Keller and Schickentanz weren't good enough to beat me in the same RSRs. So he kept trying to get me to go back to them. After Le Mans, in June, I left Loos and went back to Kremer. I then carried on with Kremer until August/September time. I think the last race I did for him was at the Norisring and I then went back to George Loos as I had started winning races for Kremer and Loos didn't like that. So he decided to stop driving himself and I finished the year with Loos who, because he stopped driving himself, was a lot, lot better. In fact, I then stayed with George Loos for the 1975 season as well. That was a very good year for us as we ran three cars and Hezemans and Stommelen drove as well.

At Imola, 1974, I remember, the scrutineers disqualified us due to our mechanics re-routing the oil pipes as they fouled a rear wheel under the wheel arch. The Italian scrutineers impounded the first three cars and disqualified them and then awarded the race to the 4th place driver who had, of course, taken his car home and they couldn't check the eligibility of his car!

Panteras and Daytonas were no opposition. Muller had a Pantera in 1972 which on occasions was quite quick. He could never get it to stay together. There was nothing really quite quick *and* reliable enough to beat the RSR.

I had a 2.7 litre RS Carrera on the road in 1973 and loved it, but in 1974 I had one of the few 3.0 litre RS lightweights on the road. I remember it being a tremendous price but what a car! It shot up in value straight away and I'd love to have one of them today.

Norbert Singer

I remember we started the 1973 season

with a normal G.T. car and I think after one or two races, at Monza. We got a protest about the bearings on the rear suspension and during the meeting, I changed the category to the prototype (group 5) which is officially not allowed, but with Herbert Muller on our side, we could do it! We raced there as a prototype. We changed the rear spoiler for the race as it was only a normal Carrera ducktail and we made it larger which made the car handle better. On that basis, we made these parts out of fibreglass for the next race and called the new spoiler "Mary Stuart" as it looked like a ruff. We raced the whole season with that shape of spoiler except for Le Mans.

In 1973 the FIA were talking about new regulations and these would be close to production cars, but these were only rough ideas. In 1974 the Turbo-Carrera was a move towards the new regulations and they said that the new regulations would start in 1975. Then nearly at the end of the season, they (the FIA) announced that the new regulations would not start until 1976 and this led us to the 935.

The idea was to have more room for development with the works Martini sponsored cars in 1973. This was really the start of us experimenting aerodynamically with the 911. I think we had at Zeltweg, in Austria, a long tailed car, it was just one of the experiments. In 1974, we offered the customers the 3 litre RSR after having made 100 3 litre RSs as a "face-lift" and the problem was that you had to have the weight of the homologated car as the actual racing weight. In other words, you had to have a light road car in order to keep the weight down on the racing car. They had fibreglass doors and thin glass and hardly any interior trim. Nobody was talking about selling cars to racing customers in the beginning (1973) for at that time, you remember, there was Kremer and other race shops running 911s in the normal G.T. class. (911Ss) and they were quite happy. But when we came in and were competing, against them, I remember at Vallelunga, the first race, in 1973, our G.T. cars were the only cars to qualify. All the others were not fast enough. Well, it was quite hard, for this was the year that the Matra was racing against Ferraris and Alfas and they were very fast. There was a rule that gave 120% in qualifying and it was quite close, so at the end, we had won the G.T. class but we were the only entrants! . . .

There was quite a bit of opposition to us in the European G.T. championship. The De Tomaso Panteras. Actually, only one Pantera was really fast, the car driven by Herbert Muller. In short races, his car lasted. In fact, his car was better than the factory entered car! When he changed over to the Carreras, he was really disappointed to start with. He told me, that his Pantera was really better than our Carrera. I said 'O.K., fine, now let's start developing a better car'. He had more horsepower in the Pantera and Herbert Muller didn't like an oversteering car. He was used to understeer from the Pantera and this was quite a change for him. We had, in 1972, a test at Paul Ricard circuit and this was the point where we started to install coil springs which were allowed in group 4. Lots of people in the factory had tried this before but there was not

119

enough room to install them. Anyway, we did put them in and with them, it made it possible to balance the car really well. The stiffness with the torsion bars set really hard was 3 kilogrammes per square centimetre with the torsion bar and with a really big one you could get 3.5 or 3.7. With the coil springs, we started with 4 then 4^1/$_2$, then 5 and we ended up with 8! (plus the 3 from the torsion bar) so it was almost solid. Herbert Muller then said that, it was beginning to be a racing car. It showed very quickly that with just the torsion bars, you could not set the car up hard enough for the track. Officially, of course, the springs were supposed to be "supplementary" so as to suit the rules and in 1974, we sold them to the customers for their RSRs.

In 1973 we tested the first 3-litre engine at Le Mans in the 4-hour race. That was a test day and we said we wouldn't use the 3-litre engine for the race because it was too weak, the wall thickness between the cylinders was too thin, but on the test it was no problem. So we tried this engine and it develops 308 bhp and it was after that we changed from a magnesium crankcase to an aluminium one. We had to make the studs further out and we had to make a metal spacer to bolt onto the crankcase to hold everything together. Anyway, the engine ran perfectly and we won the 4-hour race for G.T. cars. The engine lasted two days of practise and so we decided to try it in the race.

I don't know in which race we started with the 3-litre engine in 1973 but the customers started with the 2.8 and later on the main teams switched to the 3-litre engine (with the aluminium crankcase).

John Rulon-Miller

By 1972 I was a keen club racer in Germany and took part in many of the races involving the European G.T. Championship and culminating in class wins at Le Mans in 1976 and '77. I did the races just to be along for the ride and you must remember that some of the other guys such as Schickentanz, Fitzpatrick, Ballot-Lena, Blaton, were all racing *very* seriously.

My racing was all done in 911s. At this time, 1970-71, Porsche started supplying bigger barrels and pistons, going from 2-litres to 2.1, then 2.3 and finally up to the class limit of 2.5 litres.

In 1968 I bought a 911S and went to a driving school at Hockenheim and one of the instructors was an American. He lived nearby and he'd been racing for 15 years. He asked me back for a drink and said I should go in for some racing. So I got a driving permit and joined the local Auto club and started racing in the 911S. The only changes made were wheels and Dunlop green spot racing tyres, 5 00 L fronts and 5.00 Ms rear. That year I did probably 10 races, finishing in the middle places. 1969, I raced again – same results! 1970, the factory offered a lightweight 2.2 litre car and I bought one. By this time I was doing German national races – Nurburgring, Hockenheim and some airports.

By 1970, I was mainlining motor racing and I wanted to be a proper racer – one who had his race car on a trailer and had that car covered with sponsor's decals, so I bought a year old 2-litre swb race car. In those days there wasn't as much difference between a road going and a race 911 as there was later. The interior was simpler. It still had mats on the floor and two seats and it had a small roll-bar in back. The suspension was lowered but there was no adjustment on the roll-bars. The wheels were 6" wide and it had fibreglass wings which was a blessing as they were cheaper than steel ones, both to buy and repair and they were lighter.

The engine gave 220 bhp. Then, in 1971 I got a new car from the works. A race prepared one. They weren't then much more than a road-going car – still no great wheel arch extensions. It was a 2.3 litre car and gave 250 bhp.

In the early days, opposite lock had to be used all the time with a 911 but as the tyres got wider, so cornering limits rose. In the wet the RSR reverted to handling like a 911S and opposite lock came into play once again.

I now had to get the next grade of licence, an international one and I was collecting points for this licence – exactly what you try not to do now! So I got the licence finally in 1973. I had decided there wasn't much point in coming 5th in a local race, when, with a proper race car I could come 25th in an international race at the Nurburgring.

I know this may sound strange but if you've ever raced, you'll know what I mean.

By the end of 1972, I had met a factory employee, an American by the name of John Russell and he worked in the sports department at the factory, actually as a counter boy and taking the spares van to races. He became my source of information and worked on my car. In fact, I let him drive the car in small-time club races which made my source of information, well, better!

The factory simply referred to the 2.8 litre racer as order no. M491 and it was Erwin Kremer, a tuning shop proprietor in Cologne, who called this specification an RSR. We started off 1973 with one of these and the first race was at Zolder (60 miles length) and just a German national race. I picked the car up from the factory on the Friday before the race and retired when the oil temperature became too high. A week later there was another race at Zolder and I was 7th O.A. and 3rd in class which wasn't very brilliant.

At this point there were no more than 3 or 4 other 2.8 litre cars competing, the rest were 2.5 cars from the previous year. Obviously they were better sorted than mine! Again I had the oil temperature problem at a race at Zembach in May and then I went to the first round of the European G.T. Championship on the 13th May and by that point there were a lot between ten and fifteen RSRs at Monthlery and I was astonished there was now so much opposition. I finished up being 7th O.A. and 7th in class.

Next was Imola in June and I stopped to have the wheels tightened. At this stage the car was running on five-stud fittings instead of centre locking nuts. This was followed by a local race at Hockenheim, then Nivelles was next stop for a round of the European G.T. series and I had a very big bump. I was trying out two changes at once, which is something you want to remember not to do! I was trying new brake pads which a supplier was giving me. I had drilled transverse holes in the brake discs, a trick I had seen on racing motor cycles. I remember that it cost a fortune to drill through the hardened metal, whatever the discs had cost, the drilling was 10 times as much!

When I got to Nivelles, the factory representative came round and looked at the brakes and said no, you can't do that, they will break. He was right! I was coming down into a hairpin from the start-finish straight and as I braked, one of the front discs broke and locked up a front wheel. The car spun several times and then went backwards into the only 3 feet of armco that was to be seen for 2 miles. We loaded the car onto the trailer and returned to our base in Darmstadt and we rebuilt the car from Monday morning to Thursday night. We (John Russell, Nan, my wife and myself) then set off for Portugal, the Vila Reale circuit, the last proper road circuit in Europe. It was a great circuit and that year they only had two or three G.T. cars and so they paid us an enormous (for that time) amount of starting money in escudos.

The rest of the field was made up of very quick 2-litre sports cars. The place was too narrow to overtake, you would go over a bridge with a 3 feet high parapet on one side and a 200 feet drop into a ravine on the other and if you wanted to overtake, you went up on the pavement – turned right at the barber shop, that sort of thing. Estoril was next, another Championship event a week later.

Next was the Coppa Inter-Europa at Monza, a 6 hours event and I finished with only 4th gear. Opposition was in the form of De Tomaso Panteras as Mike Parkes was their development engineer and race team leader together with Ferrari Daytonas at Le Mans. For us privateers these were too expensive to buy and race.

1974, I was busy building a 3-litre RSR for myself. Some of the early races in 1974 I was still competing with the 1973 car. The first thing I noticed about the new 3-litre RSR was an (it seemed to me) enormous power difference. The 2.8 car had all its power at the top end whereas the 3-litre had it all the way through the rev range. It also had a different sound by virtue of the flat slides instead of the butterfly throttles fitted on the 1973 car, a much deeper, more throaty sound. The car was a lot easier to drive, both because of the even power delivery and also because there was more rubber in contact with the track. We were using 10" fronts and 14" rim sizes on the 1974 car and that went up to 16" rim width on the back.

I did Le Mans 1975, 76, 77 and 78. That race is one on its own. It's really all about speed down the Mulsanne straight. We used a special top gear there which would give us an extra 20 – 25 mph flat out. The car was reaching over 175 mph there and we would even use slightly narrower tyres to lower the wind and rolling resistance. Tyres – you could do Le Mans on five tyres. Start with fresh tyres and change the left rear once.

The fuel cost was enormous, you were talking of using 30 gallons every 2 hours so the smart privateers included a French driver in the team. He was responsible for bringing fuel sponsorship and, hopefully, some money as well. A set of rain tyres was useful, no intermediates were used as it was either raining or sunny and we kept one other set of slicks in case of punctures. 1977 – a guy I had driven for at Le Mans had had a disastrous time at Le Mans. He had changed Turbos seven times and they were £700 each!

In 1975 we retired in the 10th hour. After the first five laps something broke, a rocker I think. That got fixed but it took an hour. Went back out again but an oil line to the gearbox had fractured and that showed itself in the 10th hour. I was going down the Mulsanne straight and had just passed the kink when there was an enormous bang. I declutched, shut off the battery master switch and stopped on the grass. I still have the 5th gear. There were no teeth on it and it was completely blued! I learned from this that you couldn't go to Le Mans with anything less than perfect equipment. So, 1976, Le Mans was my only race. The car was perfect and it paid off, we won our class.

In that year, I was sharing the driving with two other friends and we decided to have an unfair advantage and so we built a qualifying 3.3 litre engine because the technology was there! We put this in the car and had it scrutineered whereupon they put the ACO seals on it.

Scrutineering at Le Mans, by the way, is a whole day at the town square, they measure everything. We went out to practise at 5 pm on the Wednesday and it was a joy to drive. You could nearly do the whole circuit in top gear, and the sound! It sounded like the difference between a Golf GTI and a Volvo F12 truck. It didn't even sound like a Porsche. We got that car round in 4 minutes and 9 seconds and no one had ever bettered 4 minutes 15 seconds in an RSR. So, we made sure we changed the engine after practice and just as we finished changing the engine and had lifted it into the back of a Range Rover, six officious looking Frenchmen in cow-gowns arrived, puffing on Gaulois. They asked us how we were and we said "ca va". Now that obviously means something is wrong when a Le Mans official is that courteous!

The Range Rover was on the other side of the transporter so they couldn't see it and we said how glad we were to see them as we had now put in the race engine and would they please put the seals on (we had had one of their other guys break the seals on the other engine: He had performed this task and left). They said 'Yes, fine, may we see your other engine?' and we said 'Oooh – that's gone back to England' (this was about 10 o'clock on Friday morning). They said 'when did you take it out?' and we replied 'About an hour ago and it's gone'. In fact the Range Rover left about 10 minutes ago, you've just missed him (the mechanic).

Meanwhile the mechanic was taking two steps backwards and one step forwards around the transporter and as soon as he was out of sight you heard the Range Rover start. Believe it or not, the scrutineers never noticed him leaving and he drove right past them!

We then said 'Ah messieurs, you can probably catch the mechanic at our hotel. He may have gone there for a wash'. They said 'Very good' and all six of these officials jumped into a minivan and followed me to our hotel. This was about 20 miles away but I must have taken them on a trip lasting 70 miles!

When I got there, I just had time to reach the reception desk and say to the receptionist, "The mechanic with the engine has just left for England, hasn't he?" to which the receptionist, (who was very bright) replied: "Oui, monsieur" within the hearing of the scrutineers who had just followed me. They wanted to follow him!

1978 Le Mans we had problems. We had broke some rockers, the hardened steel variety and then we broke the gearbox. We replaced this in the pits in 50 minutes. The factory representative stopped by and said, 'You can't do that in the time' and later he came back and said, 'I told you so – you've obviously pushed the car into the parc ferme' and we said 'No, it's back on the track!'

Erwin Kremer

I entered and drove a lot of 911s from the time they were announced. My most memorable race was in 1968 when Willy Kauhsen and I won the Spa 24 hour touring race in a 911S. We also won the touring car championship for Porsche that year. I drove from 1964 to 1972, the last year driving with John Fitzpatrick in the 1,000 kilometre race. At the Rouen race, I remember, we faced three Ferrari Daytonas from the French importer, Charles Pozzi. We had a hard race with them and John and I won the class. So Pozzi protested that our car *must* have a bigger engine than a 2.5 litre one to be so fast but the scrutineers opened up the engine on our car and showed it was under 2.5 litres!

I was nine years doing races, rallies and slaloms, about 250 – 300 events in all. I had three crashes, one at the Nurburgring in a 911 and one on Montjuich with a Carrera 910 and one other in a rally with a Ford.

The 911R was too expensive for us and that's why we started building racing 911s ourselves. I had the very first 911 here in Germany in 1964. Porsche themselves started with rallies. Gerhard Mitter drove in the European Touring car championship starting at Monza and in the same weekend I started to race the 911 for the first time here in Germany with a hillclimb in Sauerland.

I ran a garage in Cologne City, in Friedrichstrasse. I drove a 365 super 90, a '56 Carrera, then one year with a Speedster.

In those years Porsche didn't bother to race with the 911. They had too much work with the sports-racing cars. It was only private customers who raced the 911. The interest with the factory started with the RS. For all our 911s up to the RS, we would buy parts from the factory and modify the cars ourselves.

We really started developing the 2.5 litre car in 1972 with bigger wheel arches and doors made of plastic and wider wheels and tyres. Dr. Helmutt Bott was at the Nurburgring where we were racing and Dr. Furhmann, who had just been put in charge of the 911 race car project came into our pits and said 'What is that with bigger fenders?' And we said, 'We made it ourselves' and Dr. Furhmann said to Hemutt Bott, 'You must make a 911 like this for the factory team!'

I was the first person to put coil springs on a 911. I made complete sets here. In the RSR time we worked with Schrick to make the new camshafts. The valve lift was higher and we made twenty pairs. The maximum power we obtained before we used these camshafts was 323 bhp. With the Schrick camshafts it was 345 – 348 bhp. The engine did not last so long, only maybe two short races, certainly not 1,000 kilometre events. The works camshafts were for the long distance races. Ours were O.K. for the European G.T. championship races as they were generally over 150 – 200 kilometres.

I had maybe five or six RSRs. In 1974, the two car team was sponsored by Salmson and even the mechanics dressed in the company colours! Clemens Schickentanz and Paul Keller were our drivers. The year before, it was Fitzpatrick and Keller.

In 1975, we competed in the German championship as well as the European G.T. championship. Jagermeister sponsored one car, Vaillant another and Wallys Jeans the other. Tebernum and Gelo were our main competitors. The last race was at Hockenheim and there was a protest. So the engines were opened and they were O.K. The 3-litre engine was the best. We and the works experimented with 3.5 litre engines but they were never reliable

---

Nick Faure

I raced three years in the JCB historic championship for Hexagon garage, one year with a D-type Jaguar and one year with a Lister Jaguar and one year with a "Birdcage" Maserati.

The car I started with was the ex-Vic Elford demonstrator 911S. It was called the "Stuttgart Streamliner" by the *"Motor"* magazine when they did the first test at MIRA. The registration was GVB 911D and it became quite a famous car. It was classified as a saloon car (group 2) in those days and we did the International touring car races when John Fitzpatrick was in Broadspeed Escorts.

I did the first Rallycross event with it and AFN managed to turn it into a racer by getting a Carrera 6 engine to put into it – titanium con-rods and all that. I still have some of the con-rods here. I scraped together everything I had, and more, and bought the car for £4,000. A lot of money then. I did the 1968 British saloon car championship with it and I won my class first time out and I started bettering Elford's times in the car and so Porsche looked at me and said, 'Ah, this poor impoverished layabout, we'll try and help him out by running the car for the rest of the season for him.' It was really on a total shoestring. We even did the whole season on one set of tyres! We had a lot of fun. We devised a strange dry-sump affair but unfortunately every time I cornered hard, an oil pipe got pinched and the bearings ran. I sold the car in '69 to a guy from Switzerland. The car was on the market recently in bits and a chap in Crawley bought it and turned it back into its original specification.

The car was very exciting to drive. The engine revved to 8,200 rpm and gave 225 bhp. On old R7s, you can imagine the handling! The Escorts would walk around me on the corners, they were that much lighter and then I would charge off and pass them down the straights and go on to full opposite lock around the corners.

I remember one race at Cadwell Park that was particularly hectic. There was half a second covering the first five cars over the finish line! I won and everybody behind me had broken windscreens and broken headlamps as I literally filled the road chucking it sideways in front of them and peppered them with gravel. That was my first taste of really close racing.

At the Motor Show 200, I beat Charles Lucas. He won the first heat by 3 seconds and I won the second heat by about 12 seconds.

I raced Porsches in 1968, 73, 74, 75 then 1976 onwards with 934s and 935s.

1973 I was offered a drive by AFN on the strength of their remembering how I pedalled the other car in 1968. They really went to town. They bought a brand new car for me and a brand new car as a back-up, that was RGO 3L. We didn't know how reliable these things were going to be.

MYX 4L was the first Carrera ever to win a race in this country. That was up at Croft. We literally stuck a roll-bar in it and took it out and won. That was the AFN demonstrator. The lightweights hadn't arrived in this country and they were desperate to get the first round in so they converted the demonstrator into a racer. It had a sunroof and full trim!

RGO 2L and 3L turned up next week. 3L was designated the spare car. Talk about the height of luxury! RGO 2L was the 1973 2.7 RS with which I won 16 races. It was unfortunately written off on a customer demonstration with Mike Franey driving when he actually used to teach in the cars. I don't think he does that now. It went back to the factory for a new shell, and all the latest gadgetry was put on it including shorter pick-up points for the rear suspension to control the rear wheel travel which I think was a shame actually as half the fun of those days was lifting a wheel.

We took the two cars down to Castle Combe and they were identical in times, down to the last tenth of a second. We just gradually did little tweaks but we didn't work out this business of lifting wheels until 1974. It was only with the advent of the shorter trailing arms that this got sorted. Even with the RS 3.0 it still lifted its wheels. Lowering the front struts on the RSR helped though. The biggest difference with the RS 3.0 we ran was racing it on 9" fronts and 11" rear rim widths and on racing slicks. With its ordinary road wheels and tyres, Pirelli CN36s, not even P7s, it felt just like a bigger 911S. Same kind of vibrant feel, lovely sensitive steering; what a Porsche should be all about. They lost it from there on, I think. I'm very fortunate, I've just picked up a lovely 2.7 RS. I really should have bought the RS 3.0 when it was offered for sale at the end of the season for twelve grand, still, there you go.

When they really get out of shape, you get onto opposite lock and with the bottom of your hand, you just give it a flick upwards and it goes straight down the road! (you must keep your foot on the throttle though!) I remember when I used to race the 911S getting all of a twist coming out of Druids at the Motor Show 200 one year and the car was all out of line, the back end needing more lock than was available. I didn't know where I was with the steering and so I just found that by taking my hands off and giving it a flick, the car sorted itself out. I thought: "Why didn't I do that before? It's so easy".

I had several drives on the continent in RSRs and some one-offs over here. The RSR was quite different to drive from an RS. There was the power for one thing. It was another dimension. You could slide them like an RS though.

Charles Ivey had the ex-Dick Lovett car which I raced for the 1975 season. It belonged to the Stroher rum company and my mate bought the car direct from Stroher because he was so embarassed at having pranged it first time out that he got rid of it. Dick Lovett bought it and I did a season with it in Modsports races. It was sold to Charles Ivey who then developed it.

David Penell from Birmingham took one of the fourteen lightweight right-hand drive cars and had an RSR built up by Chris Moulton. It had an RSR 2.8 engine with twin plugs, etc., but featured RSR 3.0 bodywork. It was very quick. I could get it round a circuit as quick as an RSR 3.0. It didn't even have coil spring suspension. I don't reckon that made a blind bit of difference anyway.

My first taste of international racing came with an RSR. Jean Blaton, "Beurlys", asked me to drive with him in the 1975 Le Mans 24-hour race. He asked me to find a co-driver and so I rang John Cooper who was on holiday and asked him if he wanted to share the drive. I told him it would cost him £1,000 and he agreed.

The car had previously been yellow and had been used just once previously driven by myself and Richard Bond in the 1,000 kilometres race at Brands Hatch at the end of 1974 and I repainted the car in the Harley-Davidson colours. I drew a sketch of the car in the proposed colours for the Harley-Davidson people and as a joke, I gave the car the number "69". Imagine my astonishment when I got to Le Mans and found the A.C.O. had allocated the number to us!

We finished 6th overall which is the best result I've ever had at Le Mans. The car just ran and ran and we were in the pits just twenty minutes in the twenty four hours, almost a record. We didn't even change tyres! The car was sold afterwards to someone in British Guiana, a great shame as it's just disappeared off the racing scene. I should have been a bit more shrewd and bought it off Jean. The chassis number was 072.

I drove the car for the last stint, between mid-day till 4 o'clock, just one minute short of my allowance and it rained for twenty minutes. The 911RSs were really all the same to drive in the wet. They are the best car to drive in the world, I think. Just swing them around from the back!

The RSs are real classics, they were the last of the road cum race cars. The last car you could think of driving to the circuit instead of trailering it everywhere and I think if you can do that it qualifies it for the title of "Classic".